THE INVESTING KIT

Bay Gruber

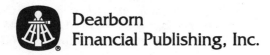
Dearborn
Financial Publishing, Inc.

Dedication

To my parents, Marjorie and George Gruber, and my brother, Renn, who have always supported and encouraged me to pursue my goals and happiness.

This publication is designed to provide accurate and authoritative information in regard to the subject matter covered. It is sold with the understanding that the publisher is not engaged in rendering legal, accounting or other professional service. If legal advice or other expert assistance is required, the services of a competent professional person should be sought.

Managing Editor: Jack L. Kiburz
Senior Associate Editor: Karen A. Christensen
Cover Design: S. Laird Jenkins Corporation
Interior Design: Lucy Jenkins

© 1996 by Dearborn Financial Publishing, Inc.®

Published by Dearborn Financial Publishing, Inc.®

Printed in the United States of America

96 97 98   10 9   8   7   6   5   4   3   2   1

Library of Congress Cataloging-in-Publication Data

Gruber, Bay.
    The investing kit / Bay Gruber.
      p. cm.
    Includes bibliographical references and index.
    ISBN 0-7931-1645-7 (pbk.)
    1. Investments—Handbooks, manuals, etc.   I. Title.
  HG4527.G78   1996
332.6–dc20   95-46018
                                                  CIP

Contents

Foreword

The reader of this book is the beneficiary of one man's odyssey— the quest for excellence as a professional money manager and a desire to help others achieve success in the increasingly complex world of investments. Bay Gruber has steadfastly held to these goals ever since he became an account executive trainee in a program I directed for what is now Dean Witter Reynolds Inc.

No one I know is more qualified to write this workbook on investing. *The Investing Kit* is a primer and guide for the individual investor unparalleled by any other single source. In addition to walking you through the process of establishing your investment goals and objectives, it offers reliable advice on managing your own portfolio. The explanations of the large variety of investment products offered in today's markets are a great plus . . . and throughout the book, Bay adheres to a "tried-and-true" teaching method—keep it simple.

So many of the books on investing are beyond the typical investor's ability to assimilate and use. Bay Gruber's belief is that a book isn't worth reading unless it provides a direct benefit to the reader. *The Investing Kit* does precisely that. And because it deals with the basics, and not the investment fads of the moment, it is timeless. I believe it deserves a prominent place in every investor's library.

Glen E. Givens
Former National Training Director
Dean Witter Reynolds Inc.

Preface

During many years of making investment recommendations to my clients, I have observed that *financial security* brings peace of mind to people. Proper investment planning and decision making take time. The process is long term. The terminology Wall Street investment firms use can be confusing and technical. The best advice is for you to take your time selecting your investment professional and the firm you want to handle your securities business. Educating yourself about portfolio management, asset allocation, diversification, individual investments, risks, returns and the trading characteristics of the different markets will provide you the avenue for financial security.

The unique feature of this book is that it contains Portfolio Investment Questions (PIQs) that you, as an investor, should answer before investing in a particular investment. By asking these key questions, you will learn nearly all of the pertinent facts about the investment. The answers will allow you to better understand the features, benefits, sales charges, expenses, risks and potential returns of the investment prior to making a purchase. This information may be kept as a reference so you can continually evaluate the investment in light of your investment objective.

The Investing Kit provides three crucial benefits: (1) It guides you in developing an investment portfolio strategy based on your investment goals, investment objectives, asset allocation and diversification; (2) it helps you become savvy about specific investments; (3) it provides you with a structured process for the investment professional to explain the necessary facts about a particular investment before you decide to invest.

Many times I have heard, "If it is worth having, it is worth working for." Financial security is worth having; therefore, it must be worth working for. Read the book, but more important, pose the Portfolio Investment Questions to your investment professional so you are better educated to make decisions about your investments. Remember, your portfolio is your financial health. Watch it, learn about it and take responsibility for understanding your investments. Ask the PIQs and you will become a more knowledgeable investor.

The Investing Kit is not meant to be a complete financial plan nor a comprehensive investment portfolio program. The introductions to the various investment areas are to provide you with a brief summary of some key points, but not necessarily all of them. Questions in addition to those listed under the Portfolio Investment Questions (PIQs) may need to be asked and understood to thoroughly comprehend investing, and the risks and potential rewards associated with an investment portfolio.

I wrote *The Investing Kit;* it is not a Dean Witter Reynolds Inc. production. I obtained the information and data from sources considered reliable, and their accuracy or completeness is not guaranteed. Individuals should consult their personal tax or legal advisers before making any tax or legal investment decisions.

Acknowledgments

Sharing several acknowledgments with you gives me an opportunity to show appreciation to those who assisted me with this book. I would like to thank and praise June A. Newell for her excellent job of editing and using her computer skills in typing the manuscript. Elizabeth A. Vetell, Richard A. Welch and James W. Sibson deserve my deep appreciation for their support and ideas in creating a better manuscript. I would also like to thank Kristine Balling for her assistance.

Sincere gratitude goes to my associates, Renn G. Gruber, Judith K. Jenkins, Cynthia M. Krupo and Marie F. Somers, who allowed me the time to write this book. Also, credit should be extended to Glen E. Givens who wrote the foreword and gave me the opportunity while I worked for him to acquire the knowledge to write this book.

Much appreciation to Caroline Carney for having the confidence in the purpose of the book and Karen A. Christensen who helped me tremendously with the editing process. Both have been a pleasure to work with.

How To Use Your Investing Kit

The Investing Kit is designed to provide you with a means to learn pertinent information about portfolio management and investments and to be able to ask key questions that will help you understand them better. The book is divided into four sections: (1) Part I on portfolio management; (2) Part 2 on investments; (3) three Appendixes, including ten Financial Focuses, eight Tax Information forms and several resources for information; and (4) a glossary of terms.

Portfolio Management and Investments

Each chapter contains three sections: (1) an introduction to the respective chapter topic; (2) Investor's Tips; and (3) Portfolio Investment Questions (PIQs).

Introductions. The introductions in the first four chapters review your investment goals, financial condition, investment objectives and tax profile. These chapters are very important because the information discusses *why you are investing* and your financial ability to invest.

The next four chapter introductions explain managing your portfolio, knowing your professional advisers, setting up your investment account and locating your important documents. Portfolio management is the foundation that allows you to become financially secure. Understanding asset allocation, diversification, risks and returns will help you establish a suitable portfolio.

The remaining 15 chapters cover types of investments, such as annuities, bonds, certificates of deposit, closed-end bond funds, mutual funds, stocks and unit investment trusts. The introductions explain the features and benefits of the various investments, along with how a particular investment fits into your portfolio.

Investor's Tips. This section lists several important ideas or caveats regarding the investment information you just read.

Portfolio Investment Questions (PIQs). The PIQs alone make this book invaluable. Some of the PIQs are designed for you to ask yourself and to record your answers, such as identifying your investment goals. You can use other PIQs to ask your investment professional so you can obtain the information necessary to making knowledgeable investment decisions. If you don't completely understand an answer, ask your investment professional to explain it again.

Each set of PIQs covers the features, objectives, sales charges, risk and return of an investment and provides other pertinent facts about the investment. You can use the PIQs threefold: (1) as a way to understand the investment better *prior to* investing; (2) as a reference guide after your purchase; and (3) periodically, or at least annually, as a valuation guide to determine whether the investment is performing in line with your objective.

Complete your PIQs each time you consider a new investment. Therefore, if you want to buy five common stocks, you need to complete five separate PIQ checklists for each stock. File the PIQs with your brokerage statements for future reference. You will need to make photocopies of the PIQs in the book in order for you to have one for all of your investments.

Financial Focuses

As an added value, the Financial Focuses target more in-depth, specific topics. Take time to read these pages in Appendix A; they will help you understand some key points when investing.

Tax Information Forms

In Appendix B, a tax information form is provided for each general investment area. Besides being required by the Internal Revenue Service (IRS), tax information is important in making appropriate investment decisions. After finalizing a purchase, complete the top portion of the corresponding tax information form. When you consider selling, refer to the tax information form to determine your potential tax liability. After you sell the investment, record the sale information and retain the form for your tax preparation. The form also allows you to record any name changes, splits or participation in dividend reinvestment programs.

CHAPTER 1

Exploring Your Investment Goals

Life is a series of setting and trying to reach goals. Achieving financial security is a vital one. As the saying goes, "If your goal is nothing, you just may achieve it." Likewise, if your goal is *financial security,* you may achieve it, too. Most people have numerous diverse goals when investing their assets. The difficult job is trying to identify and prioritize these goals and meld them into a comprehensive investment goal. Once you accomplish this exercise, you then match the appropriate investment objective to the investment goal. What makes this process even more difficult is that the investments available have several different investment objectives.

FIGURE 1.1   Ways To Organize Your Investment Goals

Goal as of 1996	Year To Achieve Goal	Current Assets	Investment Goal	Assets Needed To Reach Goal	Assets Needed per Year
College fund for daughter	2010	$2,000	$ 44,000	$ 42,000	$ 3,000
Down payment— second house	2000	2,000	20,000	18,000	4,500
Retirement fund	2031	0	500,000	500,000	14,285

Your First Step: Outline and Then Organize Your Investment Goals

The best way to outline, then organize your investment goals is to list exactly where you want to be financially in one, three, five and ten years, or longer. The list should contain not only the dollar amount you wish to accumulate, but also the purpose of the assets. Try to be as exact as possible with the numbers. Also, be as specific as you can when stating the goal of the investments—for example, build or buy a house, create a college fund, purchase a boat or car or establish a retirement fund.

Long-term goals, such as retirement or college education savings, may not have to be funded by the same amount each year if the assets increase in value. When the assets grow due to income reinvestment and capital appreciation, less money will have to be invested. However, capital losses may make it necessary for you to invest more money; otherwise, it will take longer for you to meet your goal.

Figure 1.1 illustrates a way to organize your investment goals. Revise the table annually to determine whether you are on track in reaching these goals.

Your Second Step: Calculate How Much Money You Must Invest and How Much You Will Be Able To Invest in the Future

The best way to accomplish this step is to complete the PIQs in Chapter 2. This will provide you with a list of your investments and the totals for each investment category. Then establish a budget to determine how much you can invest after all of your expenses are paid. A good method of calculating your budget is to use *The Budget Kit,* by Judy Lawrence (Dearborn Financial Publishing, Inc.). Once you figure the amount available for investing, try to set aside this money on a regular basis for investment. Regarding your investment dollars as an expense that you must pay each payday ensures that you budget a predetermined amount to be invested regularly. Experts say that this amount should be at least 10 percent of your pretax earnings.

If the amount you *must* invest and the amount you *can* invest don't match, you should still continue to invest as much as you can without jeopardizing your financial stability. Do not be tempted to pursue unduly risky investments to try to make up for the difference quickly. This strategy may cause you to lose substantial capital, which would make it even more difficult for you to achieve your investment goals. The prudent thing to do is to stay with quality investments, change your budget so you are able to invest more, and in some cases accept the fact that you may have to wait a few more years to accomplish your goal.

Your Third Step: Determine Which Investments Will Help You Achieve Your Investment Goals

People generally have three universal objectives when investing: (1) preservation of capital; (2) income from the investment; (3) increase in the value of invested capital (capital appreciation). Capital appreciation is also known as *growth.* Chapter 3 explains these basic investment objectives in more detail.

Your Fourth Step: Implement Steps One Through Three

The PIQs in the following chapters will help you focus on your investment goals (step one), calculate how much you can afford to invest (step two) and select investments with objectives appropriate to your financial goals (step three).

Your Next Step: Continual Portfolio Management

The stock, bond and other financial markets change constantly. Therefore, reevaluate and update your investment goals annually to make sure they are still in line with your priorities. Next, review the portfolio to determine whether any changes are necessary. You may also want to go through steps one and two periodically to determine whether your financial condition has changed; this may alter your investment decisions. Meeting with your professional advisers at least once a year will provide an excellent review of your financial position.

Your Portfolio Investment Questions (PIQs)

Putting your goals in writing usually helps define and prioritize them. The following PIQs provide you with a means to list your investment goals. Answer the questions as best as you can so your goals will be focused when you invest. Revising your investment goals annually helps you stay on track in meeting them. Let's take the first steps in helping you achieve financial security!

 INVESTOR'S TIPS

- The *key* to reaching your investment goals is to *begin investing* so you have some assets growing.
- Plan now; *invest* for the *future.*
- A worthwhile saying to remember is: *"Nothing ventured, nothing gained."*

Exploring Your Investment Goals

Your Portfolio Investment Questions (PIQs)   **Date** _____

1. Is your investment goal to earn enough capital to buy or build a home?

    In what time frame do you expect to achieve this?

    How much money do you anticipate needing?

2. Is your investment goal to raise your standard of living?

    How would you like to raise the standard?

3. Is your investment goal to use the income from your investments to reduce your financial dependence on your employment income?

4. Is your investment goal to earn enough capital to start a business?

    In what time frame do you expect to achieve this?

    How much money do you anticipate needing?

5. Is your investment goal to establish a college fund for your children's education?

    How many years do you have to invest for each child?

    How much money do you anticipate needing?

    Complete table on next page, if applicable.

Exploring Your Investment Goals (Continued)

Your Portfolio Investment Questions (PIQs)   Date _____

    Child 1 _____ years $ _____
    Child 2 _____ years   _____
    Child 3 _____ years   _____
    Child 4 _____ years   _____
               Total: $ _____

6. Is your investment goal to earn extra dollars for travel and vacations?

   Where do you want to travel?

   How much money do you anticipate needing?

7. Is your investment goal to achieve financial independence?

   In what time frame do you expect to achieve this?

   How much money do you anticipate needing?

8. Is your investment goal to build a substantial estate for your children?

9. Is your investment goal to build a portfolio that will provide a lifestyle acceptable to you when you retire?

   In what year do you want to retire?   Your spouse?

   How much money do you anticipate needing?

10. Is your investment goal different from those in the above questions? If so, elaborate here.

✎ Exploring Your Investment Goals (Continued)

Your Portfolio Investment Questions (PIQs)   **Date** _____

11. List your investment goals from first priority to last:

Priority of Goals	*Investment Goals*
1. _____	Buy or build a home
2. _____	Higher standard of living
3. _____	Reduce dependence on employment income
4. _____	Start a business
5. _____	College fund
6. _____	Travel and vacations
7. _____	Financial independence
8. _____	Substantial estate for heirs
9. _____	Retirement
10. _____	Other goal _____

12. List your goals from Question 11, and complete the remaining
     information below.

Organizing Your Investment Goals

Goal as of (Year) _____	Year To Achieve Goal	Current Assets	Investment Goal	Assets Needed To Reach Goal	Assets Needed per Year To Reach Goal

CHAPTER 2

Creating Your Financial Profile

Creating a *personal financial statement*, also known as a *balance sheet*, enables you to look at your entire current financial picture, including your assets, liabilities and net worth. First list both your assets and liabilities separately. Then determine your net worth.

Figuring Your Assets

Assets are those financial items that you own or that are owed to you. Assets include, but are not limited to, automobiles, cash value of insurance policies, bonds, certificates of deposit (CDs), real estate, personal items—such as clothing, furniture and jewelry—savings accounts and stocks. Another type of asset you may have is a receivable. A *receivable* is anything that a person expects to receive from another individual, such as a loan payable to you. Add the value of all your assets.

Figuring Your Liabilities

Generally, when a person owns something, he or she has either paid for it or has borrowed money to buy it. The portion that was borrowed to pay for the asset is a *liability*. Therefore, when you buy an asset such as a home, you borrow money in the form of a mortgage, which is a liability. Other liabilities include credit card balances, car loans, any money borrowed against the cash value of a life insurance policy and items that are required to be paid to a corporation, person or government, such as interest and taxes. Add all your liabilities.

Figuring Your Net Worth

To figure your net worth, subtract your total liabilities from your total assets. If your net worth is positive, you are considered solvent and in good financial condition. If your net worth is negative, you are considered insolvent and in poor financial condition. To help you prepare your balance sheet, several computer software programs are available.

Your Portfolio Investment Questions (PIQs)

Your assets and liabilities will fluctuate over time, but what is important is that your net worth increases. Therefore, you need to calculate your net worth periodically to make sure you continue to improve your financial condition. Taking time to complete the following personal financial statement will give you a good analysis of your financial condition. Knowing your net worth is an excellent way to begin to achieve your financial security. And updating your personal financial statement annually or whenever a major financial change occurs will help you track your financial condition. It can be emotionally rewarding to see your net worth grow.

Figure 2.1 will help you list the securities that you are holding. The chart consists of five columns: quantity, name of security, Committee for Uniform Security Identification Procedures (CUSIP) number, purchase date and cost basis. Quantity is important to know so you may track your purchases with the respective cost basis. When listing the name of the security, be as exact as possible with the description since many companies have similar names and different types of securities. The CUSIP number is an identifying number of publicly traded securities. The purchase date allows you to research the history of the transactions for tax purposes, splits and other company capitalization changes. The *cost basis* is the total amount you pay for a security, including transaction charges. The cost basis may be adjusted by any return of principal. Check with your tax attorney or certified public accountant (CPA) to determine your correct cost basis, which is required by the Internal Revenue Service (IRS) when selling a security. Also, in some cases when transferring securities you may need to provide the recipient with the cost basis.

 INVESTOR'S TIPS

- *Review* your financial profile *periodically.*
- Know what you are worth financially.
- The name of the investment game is to consistently *increase your net worth.*

✎ Your Personal Financial Statement

Your Portfolio Investment Questions (PIQs)   **Date** _____

ASSETS

Cash, Savings, Money Market Funds

Checking accounts	$_____
Savings accounts	_____
Money market deposits	_____
Money market funds	_____
Certificates of deposit (CDs)	_____
U.S. Treasury bills	_____
Subtotal	$_____

Investment Securities
(Use Figure 2.1 for detailed listing.)

Annuities–fixed	$_____
Annuities–immediate	_____
Annuities–variable	_____
Corporate bonds and notes	_____
Government bonds and notes	_____
Municipal bonds and notes	_____
Stocks–common	_____
Stocks–preferred	_____
Open-end (mutual) funds	_____
Closed-end funds	_____
Unit investment trusts	_____
Limited partnerships	_____
Managed futures	_____
Subtotal	$_____

🖉 Your Personal Financial Statement (Continued)

Your Portfolio Investment Questions (PIQs)   Date _____

Loans Owed to You

(Identify) #1 _____ $_____

(Identify) #2 _____   _____

Subtotal $_____

Real Estate—Market Value

Primary residence $_____

Secondary residence   _____   _____

Investment property #1 _____   _____

Investment property #2 _____   _____

Subtotal $_____

Personal Property

Auto #1 _____ $_____

Auto #2 _____   _____

Clothing   _____

Jewelry   _____

Furniture   _____

China, silver, etc.   _____

Other _____   _____

Subtotal $_____

Life Insurance Cash Value

Policy #1 _____ $_____

Policy #2 _____   _____

Policy #3 _____   _____

Subtotal $_____

Your Personal Financial Statement (Continued)

Your Portfolio Investment Questions (PIQs)   Date _____

Other Assets

(Identify) #1 _____ $_____

(Identify) #2 _____   _____

Subtotal $_____

TOTAL ASSETS $_____

LIABILITIES

Notes and Loans Payable

Auto #1 loan _____ $_____

Auto #2 loan_____   _____

Other loans _____   _____

Subtotal $_____

Accounts and Bills Payable

Credit card #1 _____ $_____

Credit card #2 _____   _____

Credit card #3 _____   _____

Credit card #4 _____   _____

Credit card #5 _____   _____

Other bills _____   _____

Subtotal $_____

Real Estate Mortgages

Primary residence $_____

Secondary residence _____   _____

Investment property #1 _____   _____

Investment property #2 _____   _____

Subtotal $_____

✏ Your Personal Financial Statement (Continued)

Your Portfolio Investment Questions (PIQs)   Date _____

Unpaid Taxes and Interest

   Unpaid taxes $_____

   Unpaid interest   _____

   Subtotal $_____

Other Liabilities

   (Identify) #1 _____ $_____

   (Identify) #2 _____   _____

   Subtotal $_____

   TOTAL LIABILITIES $_____

NET WORTH

   Total Assets $_____

   Total Liabilities (subtract)   – $_____

     TOTAL NET WORTH $_____

Notes

FIGURE 2.1   Detailed Listing of Investment Securities

Quantity	Name of Security	CUSIP Number	Purchase Date	Cost Basis

CHAPTER 3

Establishing Your Investment Objectives

"I WANT TO MAKE MONEY!" This is the most common "investment objective" investment professionals hear from their clients. It is absolutely true that people want to make money; however, the statement is not so simple: Do you want to receive money now? Do you want to receive money later? Do you want a combination of both? Do you want your money to grow quickly or slowly? What are the tax considerations when you make more money? Are you willing to lose some of your money while trying to make more? All of these questions have to be asked and answered to best achieve the "I WANT TO MAKE MONEY!" objective.

Primary Investment Objectives

Based on your age, emotional make-up, current and long-term goals, employment status, financial condition, health, income and lifestyle, your investment objectives will change over time. People invest for three primary reasons: (1) preservation of principal; (2) income from investment; and (3) increase in the value of invested capital (capital appreciation). *Capital appreciation* is also known as *growth.* Usually, investors want some income from their investments while they wait for the investments to increase in value. And even though investors may want an income-producing investment, they may still want the income reinvested in the same security. They like to see the investment increase in value by the accumulation of income earned. Therefore, one of the primary questions you must answer is *"Do you want income and/or growth investments?"*

Specific Investment Objectives

As stated in Chapter 1, people have many investment objectives. Each security has different characteristics that may meet one or two investment objectives. Let's look at the most common investment objectives: preservation of capital, income, safety of income and capital appreciation (growth).

Preservation of capital. One aim of a well-balanced portfolio is to ensure that the initial investment does not decline in value. If you are not able to replace the capital, the need for a secure investment is even more important to you. Adding "safe" financial investments to your portfolio, such as those in which the principal and interest are insured or guaranteed, may be an important step in achieving this vital investment goal.

Income. Some of the investments for a portfolio may be chosen to provide a steady stream of income. This income can be used either to meet current expenses or for reinvestment purposes. Income can add significantly to your total return.

Safety of Income. Safety of income measures the likelihood that anticipated income from an investment will continue to be paid in the amount and at the time expected. Safety of *principal* indicates that the principal value of the investment will be paid to you either at maturity or when you need it.

Capital Appreciation (Growth). An investment's value may grow, or appreciate, because of changing market conditions or due to the success of a business operation. Over the long term, the return from capital appreciation can be an important factor when you try to accumulate larger sums of money. Also, consider holding some growth-oriented investments in your portfolio to minimize inflation risk.

Investment Characteristics

Each type of investment has certain characteristics, such as liquidity, volatility and minimizing taxes, which you may want to consider when investing.

Liquidity. Liquid investments can be converted quickly into cash to realize a gain, limit a loss, take advantage of another investment opportunity or aid in an emergency. How much liquidity you need depends in part on your individual circumstances—for example, your age, health, wealth and family situation.

Volatility. Significant fluctuations in your principal value can occur in many investment areas. If you are not comfortable with volatility, you may want to consider an investment that does not fluctuate as much in value. However, the returns may be less than you want.

Tax. Taxes can affect the returns from an investment substantially. Depending on your tax bracket, your investment objective for income may be altered based on the taxability of the investment income. Most investors' objective is to reduce the tax burden by appropriate tax and investment planning.

Different Strokes for Different Folks

Because every person is unique, you will have very definite, very individual investment objectives. However, many people fall into common categories, such as the following ones:

- A *retired person* usually prefers investments that offer a good income, whereas a *young person* may want a growth-oriented investment in order to accumulate more assets for use in later years.
- A *middle-aged person* may want a combination of income and growth-oriented investments to supplement his or her salary, as well as build assets for a second home, travel or retirement.
- *Parents* and *grandparents* may invest for a child's education and use an income-oriented investment or a growth-oriented investment, depending on their market outlook and their risk aversion.
- A *person in a higher tax bracket* may want tax-free or tax-deferred income investments. (Tax bracket often dictates the types of investments a person should purchase.)

Fear and Greed

Many people experience two overriding emotions when investing: the fear of losing money and the greed of making more money. For instance, if you fear losing money, you may be reluctant to purchase higher-risk investments even though they may offer higher returns. On the other hand, you may become greedy in trying to achieve additional profits, thereby preventing you from selling an investment when the outlook appears to be changing unfavorably.

It is important for you to understand the various potential risks and rewards when investing because considering these two factors affects how and why you invest. The common way of knowing whether you are making money or losing money is to calculate a percentage return. Numbers are always interesting to figure because they can be calculated in many different ways.

Risk

Most people realize that investing is a risky business, but they often don't identify precisely the diversity of perils that a particular investment faces. When you invest, be alert to the eight major risks described below. With proper diversification, you can guard against overexposure to any one and preserve any potential long-term returns on your overall portfolio.

Inflation Risk. Inflation risk is also known as *purchasing power risk.* Rising prices will reduce the purchasing power of a dollar. For example, an annual inflation rate, as measured by the Consumer Price Index (CPI), of only 5 percent over 15 years will cut the value of $1,000 to $481. Overly cautious investors who keep all their assets in lower-yielding investments such as savings accounts and money market funds may not earn enough to outpace rising prices. In addition, rising inflation reduces the value of future income from investments with fixed-income payments, such as long-term bonds.

Interest Rate Risk. The *interest rate* is the *price of money.* When interest rates change, investors may sell one investment and buy another, making prices move. Rising interest rates cause fixed-income investments to decrease in price. Higher interest rates also make yields on existing bonds less attractive, so their market values decline. And rising rates may make stocks less attractive by making their dividend yields look less valuable and, over the long run, may hurt the profitability of the underlying companies. Investors who borrow money from brokerage firms to purchase stocks face higher borrowing costs as interest rates rise.

Economic Risk. Slower economic growth usually causes investments to fall in price. Shares of growth companies may decline because they require an expanding economy to sustain their earning gains. Cyclical companies, such as auto makers and chemical producers, usually cannot cut costs as fast as revenues decline during a recession, so their shares may decline as well. Economic downturns can also undercut low-quality bonds issued by financially weak firms that might default.

Market Risk. Market risk results from the price fluctuation of an investment. The value increases or decreases based on the supply and demand for the security. The factors causing the change in value may be real or they may be related to the expectations of buyers and sellers. Such factors as economic and governmental policies, unrest overseas, tax law changes, trade agreements, computerized program trading and the like may all contribute to market volatility. Investor psychology may also affect the performance of investment markets, both positively and negatively.

Specific Risk. Specific risk covers events that may affect only a particular company or industry. For example, the death of a young company's founder could send the stock price down. Specific risk also includes the possibility that government regulations will harm a particular group of companies, that technological advances will push an industry into long-term decline or that new competitors will force profit margins down.

Marketability Risk. Marketability risk results from a person's inability to sell or liquidate the investment into cash. If the investment has appreciated in value but cannot be sold, the value cannot be realized; thus, the investor faces the risk that the value may fall in the future. Lack of liquidity may cause the investor to accept a lower price than the true value of the investment.

Taxation Risk. Taxation risk results from the government changing the tax laws that affect a particular investment. The new tax law may cause the investment to be less profitable than it was under the old law.

Financial Risk or Credit Risk. Financial risk results from the issuer's inability to turn a profit and remain in business to meet its financial obligations. For example, with bonds, the financial risk is whether the issuer can make interest and principal payments to the bondholder. Stocks have financial risk associated with the underlying companies staying profitable and paying dividends to the shareholders.

Always consider the risk and return of an investment. *The greater the risk, the greater the **potential** return.* However, before investing, you must decide how much risk you are willing to accept.

Return

People invest in the securities markets for a variety of reasons. As discussed earlier, their investment objectives are usually preservation of capital, income and/or capital appreciation. Following are the possible returns from investing, which can be calculated by various methods. (See Financial Focus 1 in the appendix for more on calculating returns.)

Nominal Yield. Nominal yield is the annual interest rate payable on a bond. It is specified in the bond indenture (bond agreement) and printed on the face of the certificate itself. It is also known as the *coupon rate*.

Current Yield (CY)—Bonds. Current yield is the coupon rate of interest divided by the current bond price. For example, a bond selling for $1,000 with an 8 percent coupon offers an 8 percent current yield at this point in time. If that same 8 percent coupon bond were selling for $800, it would offer a 10 percent current yield to an investor at this point in time.

Current Yield (CY)—Stocks. Current yield is the annual dividend divided by the current stock price. For example, a stock that sells for $20 and pays an annual dividend of $1 per share has a 5 percent yield at this point in time. It is also called a *dividend yield*.

Yield to Maturity (YTM). The yield to maturity is the total rate of return a bondholder will receive if the bond is held to its maturity date. To compute the yield to maturity is quite complicated. However, yield to maturity returns can be approximated using a bond value table (also called a *bond yield table*) or can be determined using a programmable calculator equipped for bond mathematics calculations.

Yield to Call (YTC). The yield to call is the total rate of return a bondholder will receive if the bond is redeemed by the issuer at the first call date. The *call date* is when the issuer may purchase the bond from the bondholder at a predetermined price (*call price*), usually more than $1,000 per bond. The *indenture* is the bond agreement, which states all of the terms of the bond issue, including call dates.

Capital Appreciation or Depreciation. Capital appreciation or depreciation is the increase or decrease in the value of an investment over time. To calculate capital appreciation or depreciation, divide the amount of the increase or decrease by the beginning value and multiply by 100. This figure provides the percentage return. To annualize the percentage, multiply the percentage by 12 and divide by the number of months held. When you sell the investment, it becomes a *realized* gain or loss. As long as you still own the investment, it is an *unrealized* gain or loss.

Total Return. Total return is the annual return on an investment, including appreciation or depreciation and income. For bonds, total return is *yield to maturity* if the bonds are held to maturity. If the bonds are not held to maturity, total return is the interest received plus or minus the change of bond price. For stocks, total return is the dividends received plus or minus the change of stock price. Fees, sales charges and transaction expenses must also be subtracted to calculate an accurate net total return.

Level of Risk and Return

Because each investment comes with risk and return, it is best to determine how much risk you are willing to take and how much return you want. Some of your assets may be considered your *serious money*—money that you do not want to risk. Some of your assets may be your *investment money*—money that you want to make a good return with reasonable risk. The rest of your assets may be your *risk money*—money that you want to make a big return, but could tolerate losing some or all of it.

Figure 3.1 illustrates a sample allocation of the three various types of money. Your percentages may differ from those in Figure 3.1 based on your age, financial condition, health, investment objectives, personal preference and risk tolerance.

Figure 3.1   Types of Money

Type of Money	Percent
Risk money	5%
Investment money	70
Serious money	25

How Much Risk, How Much Return?

Two other important numbers you need to determine are (1) the amount of risk you are willing to accept on your investment money and (2) the amount of total return you expect. Are you willing to lose 5 percent, 10 percent, 15 percent, 20 percent or more while you wait to make a profit? Do you want a total return of 5 percent, 10 percent, 15 percent, 20 percent or more? What percentage return is reasonable for you?

Knowing Your Investment Objectives

When you buy real estate, the REALTOR® always emphasizes "location, location, location." *When you invest in securities, the emphasis is investment objective, investment objective, investment objective.* Once you know your objective, you are ready to make the appropriate investment selection that has the potential to meet your investment objective.

Your Portfolio Investment Questions (PIQs)

Most people have several investment objectives. If you have a good understanding of your objectives and their order of priority, it will be easier for you to make appropriate investment decisions. Also, knowing your investment objectives thoroughly, you will be able to express them to your investment professional. This will provide the professional with a sound understanding of your goals and allow him or her to make appropriate investment recommendations. The following PIQs will help you prioritize your objectives and categorize the types of money in your portfolio.

 INVESTOR'S TIPS

- Listing your *investment objectives* in order of *priority* is important in making appropriate investment decisions. You should have *one primary objective* with *one* or *two secondary objectives*.
- Timing the market is not as important as *time in the market.*
- Review and alter, if necessary, your investment objectives as your goals change, especially as you get older.

Establishing Your Investment Objectives

Your Portfolio Investment Questions (PIQs)   Date _____

1. What are your broad investment objectives? List them in order of priority (number 1 being the most important).

   _____ Preservation of capital with some income

   _____ Primarily income with capital appreciation second

   _____ A balance between income and capital appreciation

   _____ Primarily capital appreciation with income second

   _____ Primarily capital appreciation with no consideration to income

2. Which of the following statements best describes your attitude toward investment risk?

   _____ *Conservative.* You dislike risk and will invest in only the safest and highest quality investment to try to achieve a reasonable return.

   _____ *Moderate.* You are willing to take some risk and will invest in medium-quality investments to try to achieve an above-average return.

   _____ *Aggressive.* You are willing to accept risk and will invest in low-quality investments to try to achieve a high return.

3. Is tax-free income important to you?   _____ Yes _____ No

4. Is tax-deferred income important to you?   _____ Yes _____ No

5. Are you willing to allow your principal to fluctuate? _____ Yes _____ No

6. Are you willing to allow your income to fluctuate?   _____ Yes _____ No

7. Are you willing to be invested over investment cycles where you may lose some of your principal, either realized or unrealized, due to adverse market conditions?   _____ Yes _____ No

✏ Establishing Your Investment Objectives (Continued)

Your Portfolio Investment Questions (PIQs)   Date _____

8. Knowing how you categorize your investable assets helps you make more suitable choices for your money. Use the following table to categorize your assets.

Types of Money		
Type of Money	**Percent**	**Dollars**
Risk money	%	$
Investment money	%	$
Serious money	%	$

9. Knowing your risk tolerance and your expectation of return for your total portfolio helps you make investment decisions. The following table provides you with a place to write the percentage risk (amount you are willing to lose) of your total portfolio in case the investments decline in value. Also, state the total return percentage you expect to achieve. These figures are mostly for your awareness, because each individual security in your portfolio may be viewed differently regarding risk and return.

Risk vs. Return	
Your Total Portfolio	
Risk	**Return**
%	%

CHAPTER 4

Reviewing Your Tax Profile

Taxes, taxes and more taxes! Do you feel that every time you blink, you pay more taxes? When investing, tax considerations are important. In fact, it is not as important to make a good profit as it is to keep a good profit after taxes. At least if you are paying taxes, you know you are making money. Because the tax laws change constantly, it is paramount that you understand how taxes affect your income and profits.

City and State Taxes

Each city and state has its unique tax laws; therefore, city and state laws will not be discussed in detail here. Consult a tax adviser, such as a tax attorney or certified public accountant (CPA), in your area for more information regarding local, city, state and federal tax laws.

It's Tedious, but So Very Important

Tax recordkeeping is extremely important and should be one of your priorities when investing. Proper records will help you make more informed decisions, as well as assist your investment professional in advising you more appropriately.

If you organize your records initially, the follow-through is so much easier. Therefore, keep records of all purchases, stock splits, stock dividends, dividends reinvested, mergers, acquisitions, stock distributions and sales for each security for at least three years after you report the sale of that security on your tax return.

In addition, maintain year-end statements issued by brokerage firms and mutual fund companies.

Which Security Are You Selling?

When you purchase the same security at different times (known as a *lot*) and decide to sell just a portion of the shares, you can choose which ones you actually sell. Buying a *lot* means you purchase the same security at different times, thus generating different cost bases and dates of purchase. The Internal Revenue Service says that if you don't specify which lot you are selling, the agency will assume you have sold the first one purchased. Thus, FIFO (*first one in* is the *first one out*) is the standard procedure. However, if you tell your investment professional to state which lot you are selling, you may use this particular cost basis when calculating your capital gain or loss. Just instruct your broker to "sell these (quantity) shares and print on the confirmation of sale *versus purchase of trade date* (date of purchase)." Your confirmation of sale is used as verification if you are audited by the IRS.

If you sell the lot with the lower cost basis, you will incur either a large capital gain or a smaller capital loss. Likewise, if you sell the lot with the higher cost basis, you will incur a smaller capital gain or a larger capital loss. Depending on your tax situation and other realized capital gains/losses, your decision to sell one lot rather than another may be more beneficial.

Capital gain or capital loss is calculated by subtracting the cost basis from the sale proceeds. If you make money you have a capital gain;

if you lose money you have a capital loss. You need to report both capital gains and capital losses on your tax return.

Your Tax Bracket

Most people know approximately what they pay in income tax for the year. However, only a few know their tax brackets. The percentage rate is very important when making investment decisions. When you prepare your taxes each year, take a moment and calculate the tax rate that you pay on your income. Better yet, keep this chapter handy and you should have that figure.

Your Portfolio Investment Questions (PIQs)

Preparing income tax returns is one task that most people don't enjoy. However, the following PIQs will provide you with information to determine how much income you earn and just how much you pay in taxes. By completing this list, you may be pleasantly surprised about your income, but unpleasantly surprised about the amount of taxes you pay.

Use the appropriate forms in Appendix B to help you maintain the appropriate tax information for your purchases, sales, dividend reinvestment, stock splits, name changes and capitalization changes. These forms also provide you with a means to maintain records of where you purchased the security and from whom. You should update and review your tax forms at least annually or every time a change has been made to the information.

INVESTOR'S TIPS

- Knowing what you earn after taxes is one of the best ways of maximizing your net worth. Below are two examples of figuring your *after-tax return:*

  Example 1

Assuming your federal income tax bracket is	31.00%
If you earn a *taxable income* of	7.00
Less tax due (7.00 × .31)	(2.17)
After-tax return	4.83%

  Example 2

Assuming your federal capital gains tax bracket is	28.00%
If you had a *net realized capital gain* of	12.00
Less tax due (12.00 × .28)	(3.36)
After-tax return	8.64%

- Taxes may take a significant part of your profit. Be aware of the *impact of taxation* on your earnings.
- Taxes should not be the overriding factor in making investment decisions, just one of many considerations.
- Sometimes it is best to take a profit and pay taxes rather than not sell and see your investment turn into a loss.

✎ Reviewing Your Tax Profile

Your Portfolio Investment Questions (PIQs)   Date _____

	Last Year	*Current Year*
Annual Income		
1. From wages and/or salaries	$_____	$_____
2. From CDs, money market funds, etc.	_____	_____
3. From stock dividends	_____	_____
4. From taxable bond interest	_____	_____
5. From tax-free bond interest	_____	_____
6. From other investments	_____	_____
7. From Social Security	_____	_____
8. From pensions	_____	_____
9. From other retirement accounts	_____	_____
10. Annual imputed income (e.g., OID—original issue discount)	_____	_____
11. From other sources	_____	_____
Total Income	$_____	$_____
Total Income Taxes Paid	$_____	$_____
Tax Rates (Percentage)		
12. Federal income tax bracket	_____%	_____%
13. State income tax bracket, if applicable	_____	_____
14. City income tax bracket, if applicable	_____	_____
15. State intangible tax rate, if applicable	_____	_____
16. State tangible tax rate, if applicable	_____	_____
Gains and Losses		
17. Realized capital gains	$_____	$_____

✏️ Reviewing Your Tax Profile (Continued)

Your Portfolio Investment Questions (PIQs)   Date _____

18. Realized capital loss   _____   _____

19. Capital loss carryover   _____   _____

20. The following table provides a place to record your federal income tax bracket for last year and this year for easy and quick access.

Your Tax Bracket	
Year	**Tax Bracket**
Last year	%
Current year	%

CHAPTER 5

Managing Your Portfolio

Portfolio management is the process of structuring and continually adjusting your investment assets to create a profitable portfolio appropriate for your age, financial needs and investment goals. Monitoring the economy, marketplaces and your individual securities is an ongoing process year in and year out. Your investment objectives and type of portfolio dictate how often and detailed the monitoring—and adjusting—need to be.

Some investors purchase securities for long-term capital appreciation or for fixed, steady income. Others trade securities for short-term profits. The quality of the investments may influence how much time is required to monitor the securities. The investment mix of different types of securities and asset categories provides you the opportunity to accomplish your investment objectives and earn a desirable rate of return on the dollars invested.

Allocation of Assets

Two areas are paramount to managing your portfolio: (1) allocation of assets and (2) diversification of assets, which we will discuss later in the chapter. *Allocation of assets* is an investment planning strategy whereby a portfolio is invested in several different market categories. Specific market categories react differently to changing economic environments. Each market has unique characteristics that mirror the investment climate of that category. Bonds, CDs, commodities, real estate and stocks all react differently to a particular economic scenario. Unfortunately, investor predictions and economic expectations sometimes cause the markets to change contrary to accepted analysis.

As discussed in Chapter 3, you have different levels of risk and return expectation. The percentages you specified for your serious money, investment money and risk money help determine how to allocate your assets. If you specified a high percentage for your serious money, you might allocate more assets to CDs, money market funds and fixed annuities. If you specified a high percentage for your investment money, you might allocate more assets to stocks, bonds and variable annuities. If you specified a high percentage for your risk money, you might allocate more assets to speculative-type stocks and bonds and managed futures funds. Of course, you must be comfortable with the percentages you select for the type of money and the asset allocation mix.

By allocating a certain percentage of your investment dollars to several different markets, the total return over time is generally more stable than it would be if 100 percent of the dollars were invested in one market category. Thus, a major downturn in one market will not significantly affect your total assets. On the other hand, a major upturn in one market will not affect your total assets significantly either. Also, it is usually beneficial to diversify your assets within each market category by investing in several types of securities.

Asset Categories

Most traditional asset allocation models use three broad categories: (1) money market securities, (2) bonds and (3) stocks. *Money market securities* include CDs, money market funds, U.S. Treasury bills and any short-term (less than one year) debt security. Money market securities are also known as *cash equivalents* because they can be readily converted into cash without undue risk of principal.

Alternative methods of owning *bonds* and *stocks* include open-end funds (mutual funds), closed-end funds and unit investment trusts. These methods of ownership fall in the bond and stock categories.

Managed futures, which are discussed in Chapter 22, recently have been added as an acceptable fourth category of asset allocation in some studies. Real estate and annuities may also be included as additional categories.

Sample Asset Allocation Models

Portfolio models are infinite. Because no one correct model exists, several different models may be suitable for you. Basically, using asset allocation and diversification increases the probability that your portfolio will provide you with the expected return without substantial risk.

Many academic studies show theoretical asset allocation models based on risk and reward. Using the textbook models is a good place for you to begin the asset allocation process. However, your asset allocation model should be based on your age, financial resources, health, investment objectives and personal preference. You may feel comfortable in only three or four categories and not all six. Furthermore, you should invest only in asset categories that you believe are right for you and that you are comfortable with.

Figure 5.1 displays two sample asset allocation models for investors whose investment objective is primarily income or primarily capital appreciation, based on the three traditional asset categories: money market securities, bonds and stocks. Most investors want some combination of both income and capital appreciation.

Figure 5.2 displays two asset allocation models for investors whose investment objective is either primarily income or primarily capital appreciation, based on six asset categories. Most investors want some combination of both income and capital appreciation.

Figure 5.1   Two Sample Asset Allocation Models Based on Three Categories

Investment Objective: Capital Appreciation	Asset Category	Investment Objective: Income
60%	Stocks	30%
35	Bonds and notes	60
5	Money market securities	10
100%	**Totals**	100%

Five Steps to Managing Your Portfolio

Structuring and managing your portfolio is a long-term process. It is not just deciding that you want to invest and buy different securities because they sound good and appear to be potentially profitable. Structuring your portfolio is like building a house. When you build a house, the basic procedure is to select the architect and builder, design the house, choose the materials and devise a time schedule for completion. It is not a quick and easy process. Similarly, when you build an investment portfolio, you should select the investment professional, design the portfolio, choose the securities and create a time schedule to make the investments. Your house needs to fit your lifestyle and meet your personal needs. Likewise, your portfolio needs to fit your investment objectives and meet your financial needs. The following steps should help you design your investment portfolio.

1. Allocate Your Assets. The first step in managing your portfolio is to determine what market categories you want to invest in. Of course, by now you have determined your investment goals, financial condition and investment objectives. For example, you may want to allocate your assets among the following six market categories: (1) money market securities; (2) annuities (3) real estate; (4) bonds; (5) stocks; and (6) managed futures.

Figure 5.2   Two More Sample Asset Allocation Models Based on Six Categories

Investment Objective: Capital Appreciation	Asset Category	Investment Objective: Income
10%	Managed futures	5%
40	Stocks	20
15	Bonds and notes	40
10	Real estate	5
15	Annuities	20
10	Money market securities	10
100%	**Totals**	100%

2. Define Your Percentages. The second step is to determine what percentage of your total assets you want to invest in each market category. This step is extremely important for two reasons: (1) the majority of the portfolio's total return is based on the asset allocation and (2) the allocation depends directly on your investment objective.

The percentages will vary for each individual, so it is difficult to provide an exact asset allocation recommendation. However, you may use one of several models initially. Once you have a basic allocation, you may want to revise it to make it more suitable to your investment objectives. Depending on the amount of investable assets, you may not be able to efficiently invest in all categories. You may want to begin with only a few categories, adding to the other ones as you invest additional money.

3. Decide on an Investment Method. As previously mentioned, several methods of investing exist. You may want to use most of the methods available to you. You can purchase annuities (fixed and variable), CDs, money market funds, individual securities (stocks and bonds), open-end funds (mutual funds), closed-end funds, unit investment trusts and limited partnerships. You may also want to establish a managed money account. Selecting various investment methods gives your portfolio added diversification. Each investment method has different advantages and disadvantages.

4. Select the Particular Investments—Diversify. Selection of the particular investments is key because these investments will provide you with income, capital appreciation or loss. This step relates directly to your investment objective. The quality of the security is important here. Analyze the annuity, bond, CD, money market fund or stock to determine whether it is appropriate for your portfolio. If you select a closed-end fund, mutual fund, limited partnership or unit investment trust, evaluate the fund manager (or sponsor) and the fund's investment objective. If you are going to use a managed money account, know the manager's investment style and discipline, among other things.

The best time for you to diversify is when you select your investment method. Decide how many individual securities, mutual funds (or other types of funds) and money managed accounts are appropriate for you.

Diversification is an investment planning strategy that helps reduce risk by spreading your investment dollars among many market categories, as well as among many specific investments within each category. Each market category requires a different number of securities for it to be considered diversified. Refer to Financial Focus 2 for further explanation of the benefits of diversifying.

Does a perfect investment exist? No. Investment professionals state that there is no such thing as a single ideal investment. This certainly is true because each individual investment has different sets of characteristics and various tradeoffs. These tradeoffs may or may not make the investment suitable for you.

Analyze the following investment characteristics to determine how they affect the investment objective of your portfolio: (1) safety of principal; (2) income; (3) growth of income; (4) capital growth; (5) marketability; and (6) tax benefits. One investment may have two or three of these characteristics, but generally none will have all six. Therefore, you should diversify among many different types of investments to try to achieve your overall investment objective. As a whole, however, a well-designed investment portfolio can offer you many characteristics of an ideal investment.

Difference between allocation and diversification. The major difference between allocation and diversification is that allocation refers to the *percentage* invested in each security or market category, whereas diversification usually refers to the *number* of securities or markets. Determining the percentage of your total assets to invest in each market category is a goal in itself. Many academic studies have been performed in an attempt to establish the *optimum percentages* to be allocated in the different market categories.

5. Finally, Invest and Review. Once you have chosen your asset allocation and investment selections, it is time to invest accordingly. You may invest immediately or gradually over a period of time. Do whatever makes you most comfortable. Also, market conditions may influence when and how you should invest.

Whether you invest for long term or short term, investing is not a one-time event. You must continually review, reevaluate and adjust your portfolio when appropriate. See Financial Focus 3.

Summary—Allocation of Assets

Figure 5.3 shows one example of how assets may be allocated among six categories. Below each category are several classifications of securities and investments. A broad spectrum of different types of securities with different investment objectives is listed within this allocation of assets. Not all of the different types of securities may be appropriate for you, but it may be beneficial to at least consider most of them.

However, It's Your Money

You do not have to make all of your decisions about asset allocation and diversification by yourself. Your investment professional will give you insight on allocation of assets, diversification, management styles, performance figures, quality ratings, market outlook and other investment information. Meeting with him or her on a regular basis will help you manage your portfolio better, and hopefully more profitably.

FIGURE 5.3 Sample Allocation of Assets

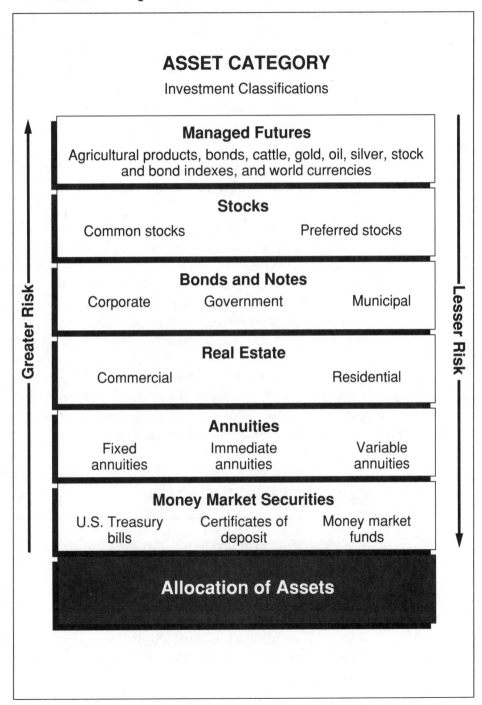

ASSET CATEGORY
Investment Classifications

Greater Risk → **Lesser Risk**

Managed Futures
Agricultural products, bonds, cattle, gold, oil, silver, stock and bond indexes, and world currencies

Stocks
Common stocks   Preferred stocks

Bonds and Notes
Corporate   Government   Municipal

Real Estate
Commercial   Residential

Annuities
Fixed annuities   Immediate annuities   Variable annuities

Money Market Securities
U.S. Treasury bills   Certificates of deposit   Money market funds

Allocation of Assets

However, *it is your money,* so invest it the way you choose. Furthermore, you have every right to ask your investment professional questions about the investments you own or are going to buy. The job of the investment professional is to give you recommendations. Make use of the ideas and expertise, but also understand why the professional recommends a particular investment and how the investment will benefit you. If you don't understand *what* you are buying or *why* you are buying a particular investment, ask questions until you do.

Your Portfolio Investment Questions (PIQs)

Make your money work for you so you don't have to work for your money! To help you achieve this goal, create a written blueprint of your portfolio to determine the proper asset allocation and diversification of securities. In this blueprint, determine how you want to allocate your assets *generally* and what diversification methods you want to use. When you need further assistance, your investment professional will help you analyze and determine *specifically* the appropriate allocation and diversification for you. To better understand the recommendations your investment professional makes, have your adviser answer the following Portfolio Investment Questions. If the recommendations do not seem to fit your needs and objectives, you may want to interview another investment professional before you invest.

 INVESTOR'S TIPS

- For the long-term investor, *asset allocation* is key to smart investing.
- Generally, the foundation of asset allocation is investing at least a *small amount* in several categories, with emphasis in a few major ones.
- Your asset allocation must conform to your age, health, financial condition, *investment objectives* and *risk tolerance.*

✏️ Managing Your Portfolio

Your Portfolio Investment Questions (PIQs)   Date _____

1. What asset allocation categories do you recommend for me?

2. What percentage should be allocated to each category?

3. What are your reasons for this allocation?

4. What methods of buying securities do you recommend? Check all that apply.

   _____ Individual securities   _____ Fixed annuities

   _____ Open-end funds (mutual funds) _____ Immediate annuities

   _____ Closed-end funds   _____ Variable annuities

   _____ Unit investment trusts   _____ Managed money account

   _____ Partnerships   _____ Managed futures funds

                                        _____ Other_____

5. What particular individual securities (stocks and bonds) do you recommend, if any?

6. What particular open-end funds (mutual funds), closed-end funds and unit investment trusts do you recommend, if any?

7. What particular fixed annuities do you recommend, if any?

8. What particular immediate annuities do you recommend, if any?

9. What particular variable annuities do you recommend, if any?

10. What managed futures funds do you recommend, if any?

11. Do you recommend using a managed money account?_____Yes _____ No

Managing Your Portfolio   (Continued)

Your Portfolio Investment Questions (PIQs)   Date _____

   If so, what is the procedure for searching for and selecting an investment manager?

12. What type of brokerage account do you recommend?

13. How should the investments be diversified?

14. How many different investments should be purchased in each asset category?

15. How will your asset allocation recommendation help meet my investment goals?

16. Is your asset allocation recommendation best suited for me, or is it your standard one?

17. How long have you used this asset allocation recommendation with other clients?

18. What economic scenario will cause the value of my total portfolio to increase?

19. What is the expected gain (total return) I might earn if I implement your portfolio recommendation?

20. What economic scenario will cause the value of my total portfolio to decrease?

21. How will the portfolio recommendation respond to declining market conditions?

Managing Your Portfolio (Continued)

Your Portfolio Investment Questions (PIQs)   Date _____

22. How do you and your investment professional want to establish your asset allocation model? (The following worksheet displays most of the investment classifications within each of the six asset categories. After reviewing your specified percentages for your types of money in Chapter 3 and your asset allocation models in this chapter, insert the percentages you feel are appropriate for your portfolio. Discuss these numbers with your investment professional. If you think it is necessary, review your investment objectives again. This is usually just a starting point. You will revise the allocation as your investment objectives change and as you become more knowledgeable.)

ASSET CATEGORY
Investment Classifications

_____% **Managed Futures**
Agricultural products, bonds, cattle, gold, oil, silver, stock and bond indexes, and world currencies

_____% **Stocks**
Common stocks   Preferred stocks

_____% **Bonds and Notes**
Corporate   Government   Municipal

_____% **Real Estate**
Commercial   Residential

_____% **Annuities**
Fixed   Immediate   Variable
annuities   annuities   annuities

_____% **Money Market Securities**
U.S. Treasury   Certificates of   Money market
bills   deposit   funds

= 100% Total Allocation of Assets

Greater Risk →
Lesser Risk →

CHAPTER 6

Knowing Your Professional Advisers

Everyone wants to be on a winning team. Get *your* team together!

It doesn't really matter whether you have ever played sports. We can appreciate good teamwork in any aspect of life. When it comes to creating your financial security, it is very important to have the right team support you and advise you on the best way to achieve your financial goals.

Building Your Team

Nowadays, companies often try to be everything to everyone. And in many cases, financial firms do offer very good comprehensive services. At the same time, numerous professions specialize only in their own lines of work—perhaps providing greater expertise. Whomever you choose, you may want to build the team of specialists that can accomplish your goals most expeditiously.

What would you do if you were the coach for the United States Olympic basketball team and had to select the players? You would probably select the two best guards, the two best forwards and the best center you could find. This would be your basketball team.

The same thing is true when you select your professional advisers. You want the best person for a particular job. Look for a person whom you can communicate with, trust and depend on and whose professional advice coincides with your objectives. You want to be confident that your adviser will give you the proper information and has the expertise to advise you.

Before you select someone for the job, interview several people in that particular profession and choose the person with whom you are most comfortable. Of course, some of the professionals may be able to perform one or two services. However, many times you want an adviser from each area who can work with your other advisers efficiently and easily.

Your Portfolio Investment Questions (PIQs)

A good way to run your team is to share the names of your investment professionals with each other. Sharing this list will help the professionals make better recommendations because they'll know who to call, when necessary, to learn more about your current situation.

The name of and pertinent information for each professional should be accessible to you so you can make decisions in a timely fashion. The PIQs that follow provide an excellent opportunity for you to list your professional team.

 INVESTOR'S TIPS

- The key to selecting your advisers is to find professionals who are both *trustworthy and knowledgeable.* One quality without the other is not good enough.
- Ask your prospective professional for three references.

✎ Knowing Your Professional Advisers

Your Portfolio Investment Questions (PIQs)   Date _____

1. Who is your stockbroker, investment adviser or financial planner?

   Name   _____

   Firm   _____

   Address _____ Telephone number _____

   _____ Fax number   _____

2. Who is your accountant or certified public accountant (CPA)?

   Name   _____

   Firm   _____

   Address _____ Telephone number _____

   _____ Fax number   _____

3. Who is your life insurance agent?

   Name   _____

   Firm   _____

   Address _____ Telephone number _____

   _____ Fax number   _____

4. Who is your health insurance agent?

   Name   _____

   Firm   _____

   Address _____ Telephone number _____

   _____ Fax number   _____

5. Who is your property/casualty insurance agent?

   Name   _____

   Firm   _____

   Address _____ Telephone number _____

   _____ Fax number   _____

Knowing Your Professional Advisers (Continued)

Your Portfolio Investment Questions (PIQs)   Date _____

6. Who is your attorney?

   Name _____

   Firm _____

   Address _____ Telephone number _____

   _____ Fax number   _____

7. Who is your banker or credit union representative?

   Name _____

   Firm _____

   Address _____ Telephone number _____

   _____ Fax number   _____

8. Who is your employee benefits counselor?

   Name _____

   Firm _____

   Address _____ Telephone number _____

   _____ Fax number   _____

9. Who is your spouse's employee benefits counselor?

   Name _____

   Firm _____

   Address _____ Telephone number _____

   _____ Fax number   _____

10. Who is your primary care physician?

   Name _____

   Firm _____

   Address _____ Telephone number _____

   _____ Fax number   _____

✏️ Knowing Your Professional Advisers (Continued)

Your Portfolio Investment Questions (PIQs)   Date _____

11. Are you satisfied with your team members? _____ Yes _____ No

> *If not,* arrange an appointment with that particular adviser to review your situation and make any necessary changes.

> *If so,* arrange an appointment with your advisers to discuss your situation to review and reiterate your financial security goal.

12. Below is a roster to complete with the names of members of your professional team.

Your Professional Team	
Professional Category	**Professional Adviser for You and Spouse**
Investments	
Taxes	
Life insurance	
Health insurance	
Property/casualty insurance	
Legal	
Banking	
Employee benefits	
Primary health care	
Other–	

CHAPTER 7

Setting Up Your Investment Account

Investment performance may be first in importance, but the quality of the investment professional and firm through which you transact business is a very close second.

The best advice is for you to take your time selecting your investment professional and the firm you want to handle your securities business. Your portfolio is your financial health. Watch it, learn about it and take responsibility for knowing your investments.

Types of Accounts

Investment (brokerage) firms offer several types of accounts. The two most common ones are regular and central assets accounts.

Regular accounts. A regular account allows you to purchase and sell stocks, bonds, mutual funds and other securities, in addition to providing other services. For example, the account might have a money market fund, where any monies deposited in the account may be swept into the money market fund. Another important service is the collection of dividends and interest from securities that are held in the account. The brokerage firm will pay you the income received or invest it in your money market fund account. Typically monthly statements report valuations of the securities in the account, indicated income from the securities and all transactions.

Central assets accounts. A central assets account is a premier account that may offer additional services to the basic account, such as checkwriting, a debit card, extra reporting statements, travelers checks, credit card protection service and additional account insurance. Typically, an annual fee is charged for the central assets account. The purpose of the account is to consolidate your financial accounts for better investment management and accountability.

Establishing an Investment Account

The first thing you must do before buying or selling securities is to open an investment account, also known as a *brokerage account*. Most brokerage accounts can hold nearly all of the investments reviewed in this book. Discuss with your investment professional the requirements of safekeeping the securities and the procedures for dividend reinvestment.

Your investment professional will ask you questions regarding your personal data (name, address, Social Security number, etc.), employment status, income, financial assets, investment experience and investment objectives. The investment professional is required to "know you" so he or she can make suitable recommendations. Providing as much information as possible about yourself will assist the investment professional in making a suitable portfolio recommendation. It will also enhance your business relationship. The brokerage firm keeps all information you provide confidential.

Brokerage services are offered by national and regional investment firms, some commercial banks and some financial planning firms. The types of services provided are usually classified by the way investors pay for the services. Brokerage services are usually provided by three entities: full-service firms, discount firms and mutual fund companies.

Full-Service Firms vs. Discount Firms vs. Mutual Fund Companies

So many choices and so much advertising. You must choose the appropriate firm for your investment needs and objectives.

Full-Service Firms. Full-service firms provide diverse investment services. Besides these services and access to professional advice, the availability of research reports is a major benefit that usually differentiates a full-service firm from a discount firm. Research reports contain financial information and recommendations for individual stocks, analyze various industries and provide an economic outlook for the country. Other basic services include execution of orders, safekeeping of securities, transfer and reregistration of securities, and dividend collection. Most full-service firms offer central asset accounts, which provide features such as checking, debit cards, expanded monthly statements and taxable and tax-free money market sweep accounts. These firms also provide investment consulting services to help you establish a managed money account. (The managed money account will be discussed in Chapter 23.) Most firms offer their own "family" of mutual funds and other propriety investment products. In addition, they offer mutual funds and unit investment trusts owned or promoted by outside companies. Besides giving personal consultations, the investment professionals at full-service firms have access to numerous computerized portfolio analysis programs. These programs can be used to help you with your financial planning, securities management and asset allocation.

Discount Firms. Discount firms provide some of the same basic services as full-service firms, such as order execution, safekeeping of securities and dividend collection. Many discount firms also offer the central asset account with standard features. Services such as computerized portfolio management programs and limited research may be available. The word *discount* is used because these firms generally charge lower commission than full-service firms when transacting orders. Discount firms are able to charge lower commissions because they offer limited services.

Mutual Fund Companies. The mutual fund groups provide direct access to them through toll-free numbers. Typically, you make all investment decisions. You must decide what type of fund to buy, when to buy it and when to sell it. You develop your own portfolio and continually monitor it. The benefit of using this method to do business is that the cost for transactions is relatively low or nonexistent. Of course, all mutual funds have management fees and other expenses.

Over the past few years, online computer services have offered investors access to some investment services.

Fee-Based Firms

Some firms, such as financial planning firms, charge a fee based on the assets under management or the assets reviewed. The fee may be a percentage of the assets or a flat fee depending on account size. Brokerage firms offer some services based on a fee rather than a commission.

Whose Street Name?

Securities bought and held in a brokerage account are considered *long* in the account and held in *street name*. This safekeeping service provides security of your holdings and easy access if you want to sell them. Usually the brokerage firm receives on your behalf all materials the company mails to shareholders. The firm then forwards the information to you.

Some securities are delivered in certificate form, while other securities are issued in *book-entry* (BE) form, meaning no physical certificate exists. The record of ownership is on the brokerage firm books at the Depository Trust Company (DTC), the central clearing agent for brokerage firms and banks. Almost every publicly traded security has an identifying number called a Committee for Uniform Security Identification Procedures (CUSIP) number. It is always helpful to supply your investment professional with the CUSIP numbers of your securities holdings, if held in your possession.

Payments and Deliveries

The brokerage firm must be paid for securities purchased within three business days (*settlement date*). Securities sold must be delivered to the brokerage firm within three business days (settlement date), and upon receipt, the brokerage firm will pay you the proceeds or credit your account. The date on which the security is executed (bought or sold) is called the *trade date.* If you hold the securities at the brokerage firm and keep sufficient balances in the money market fund, it is unlikely you will be late in making payments for or deliveries of securities when buying and selling. A late payment fee may be charged if you settle trades after three business days. When presenting the certificate for sale, you must endorse it in the proper place, exactly as the name(s) is (are) registered on the certificate.

The Fed

The Federal Reserve Board (the Fed) regulates the payments of securities purchased and sold. For securities purchased in a *cash* account, you must pay 100 percent of the purchase cost. An account is considered a cash account unless you have signed *margin* papers allowing you to pay only part (50 percent) of the purchase cost. You may borrow the remaining portion from the brokerage firm. Thus, a margin account permits the brokerage firm to loan you money by using the securities held in the account as collateral for the loan. Of course, the brokerage firm charges you interest on the amount of money borrowed.

Types of Registrations

You must sign specific documents to establish a particular account registration, such as an individual account, a joint account, a trust account, a custodial account, an individual retirement account (IRA), a corporate account, a pension account and a profit-sharing account. The firm may also require you to sign other documents and prove suitability to trade certain types of securities.

What Is SIPC?

The Securities Investor Protection Corporation (SIPC), created in 1970 by Congress as a nonprofit, membership corporation, protects securities customers of member broker-dealers. If a member firm fails financially, SIPC asks a federal court to appoint a trustee to liquidate the firm and protect its customers. The trustee and SIPC may arrange to have some or all customer accounts transferred to another SIPC member broker-dealer. If the accounts cannot be transferred to another member firm, SIPC ensures that the customers receive all securities registered in their names. Most types of securities held in the account, such as stocks, bonds and CDs, are insured up to a maximum of $500,000, including up to $100,000 in cash, excluding money market funds (as distinct from claims for securities). However, SIPC protection does not cover decline in the market value of securities. For a more comprehensive explanation of SIPC, contact the Securities Investor Protection Corporation. See Appendix C, "Resources," for the address.

Understanding the Documents You Receive

You will receive statements, confirmations of trades, financial reports, prospectuses and other documents regarding your account and the securities in it. *It is your money!* If you don't understand something, ask your investment professional to explain it. Financial documents can be confusing; however, if you read them carefully, line by line, you should be able to understand the information provided. It is well worth your time to do so.

Your Portfolio Investment Questions (PIQs)

Many financial service firms and investment professionals are available to you. Both your firm and professionals are important to your financial well-being. The following PIQs are interview questions that may help you select the right matches for you. Question 21 is an evaluation form to assist you in rating the investment professional, the firm and the services provided.

 INVESTOR'S TIPS

- The securities markets are like the weather: Some days are good and some days are bad. Consequently, you should find a *brokerage firm* and *investment professional* who will be there for you when the markets are *up* and who will weather the storms with you when the markets are *down.*
- Choose a *financially sound* firm and a knowledgeable and experienced investment professional.
- You want to be confident in your investment professional and financial service firm.

✏️ Setting Up Your Investment Account

Your Portfolio Investment Questions (PIQs)   Date _____

1. How may I obtain an annual report or other financial information on your firm?

   Name _____

   Firm _____

   Address _____ Telephone number _____

   _____ Fax number   _____

2. What is your experience and training as an investment professional?

3. How long have you worked in this industry?

4. What is your title?

5. What is your college education?

6. How many clients do you currently serve?

7. How many investment firms have you worked for?

8. What is your investment philosophy?

9. What type is your investment firm? (Check one.)

   _____ Full service   _____ Mutual fund company

   _____ Discount   _____ Fee based

10. How are commissions or fees calculated?

✏ Setting Up Your Investment Account (Continued)

Your Portfolio Investment Questions (PIQs)   Date _____

11. What type of registration is the investment account? (Check one).

   _____ Individual

   _____ Joint tenants with rights of survivorship (JTWROS)

   _____ Joint tenants in common (JTIC or TIC)

   _____ Living trust

   _____ Custodian account for minors (UGMA or UTMA)

   _____ Individual retirement account (IRA)

   _____ Simplified employee pension plan (SEP)

   _____ IRA rollover

   _____ Corporate

   _____ Corporate pension plan

   _____ Corporate profit-sharing plan (P/S plan)

12. What type is the brokerage account? (Check all that apply.)

   _____ Cash   _____ Regular

   _____ Margin   _____ Central assets

13. Does Securities Investor Protection Corporation (SIPC) insurance or some other insurance cover the account?

14. What is the cost of maintaining the account?

15. How often are statements issued?

16. What do the statements show?

17. Will you review a sample statement with me?

18. When are dividends, which are received in the account, mailed out or credited to the account?

✏️ Setting Up Your Investment Account (Continued)

Your Portfolio Investment Questions (PIQs)   Date _____

19. How often are deposits and income from investments swept into the money market fund?

20. Is a checkwriting service provided with the account?

21. Three major considerations should be made when opening a brokerage account: (1) the investment professional; (2) the firm; and (3) the type of account. Following is a brief checklist for evaluating each.

Evaluation Form				
Investment Professional	**Excellent**	**Good**	**Fair**	**Poor**
Investment philosophy				
Experience				
Length in business				
Education				
Trustworthiness				
Personality				
Investment Firm				
Financial soundness				
Reputation				
Number of services offered				
Type of Account				
Regular				
Central assets				
Services				
SIPC insured				

CHAPTER 8

Locating Your Important Documents

"Where is it when I need it?" Have you ever said these words?

Knowing the location of your important documents can be vital to both your physical health and your financial health. If something serious happens to you, your family and friends will need access to your documents to perform necessary duties for you. Time and ease of obtaining the proper information may be of the essence.

Avoid Surprises

Even during your daily, routine decision making, as well as continuing your portfolio investment review, it is necessary to obtain certain financial information to make appropriate decisions. For example, you don't want to be surprised next year when you do your taxes and find that you owe a substantial amount of money to the IRS due to a big investment gain. This may occur if you cannot find the right information regarding cost basis.

Your Portfolio Investment Questions (PIQs)

Taking care of documents is a necessary task. A little organization now may help prevent larger, costlier and more time-consuming problems later. Some people like lists, some don't. However, the following PIQs, designed as a checklist, may help during those times when you need to produce the proper piece of paper quickly.

 INVESTOR'S TIPS

- Organization is always helpful, especially when your important papers are involved.
- Your important documents should be organized and kept in a single safe place, such as a safe-deposit box or a fireproof home safe.
- Your children or heirs should be informed as to where your papers are located and should have access to them in case of emergency.
- Brokerage firms provide safekeeping and valuation services, typically free of charge or for a nominal fee.

Locating Your Important Documents

Your Portfolio Investment Questions (PIQs)   Date _____

Family Documents   **Location**

1. Will   _____

2. Living will   _____

3. Trust agreement   _____

4. Durable power of attorney (for financial management) _____

5. Durable power of attorney (for health care)   _____

6. Family medical records   _____

7. Organ donor card   _____

Property Documents

1. Deed to primary residence   _____

2. Mortgage to primary residence   _____

3. Deed to other property   _____

4. Mortgage to other property   _____

5. Title to automobile #1 _____   _____

6. Loan to automobile #1 _____   _____

7. Title to automobile #2 _____   _____

8. Loan to automobile #2 _____   _____

Insurance Documents

1. Homeowners insurance   _____

2. Other property insurance   _____

3. Automobile #1 insurance _____   _____

4. Automobile #2 insurance _____   _____

5. Health insurance   _____

6. Life insurance   _____

7. Other insurance policies   _____

✏️ Locating Your Important Documents (Continued)

Your Portfolio Investment Questions (PIQs)   Date _____

Financial Documents   **Location**

1. Bank statements   _____

2. Credit union statements   _____

3. CDs and savings accounts statements   _____

4. Credit card statements   _____

5. Investment account statements (brokerage accounts) _____

6. Mutual fund statements   _____

7. Stocks and bonds (other securities) certificates   _____

8. Annuity contracts   _____

9. Pension and/or profit-sharing statements   _____

10. Other financial statements   _____

Tax Returns

1. Prior year's tax return   _____

2. Current year tax information   _____

Valuables

1. Safe-deposit box   _____

2. Safe-deposit box key   _____

3. Safe (inform only someone you can trust)   _____

4. Combination to safe (give only to someone
     you can trust)   _____

Notes

CHAPTER 9

Mastering Money Market Funds

More than $700 billion are invested in money market funds, according to IBC's *Money Fund Report*. A *money market fund* offered by a brokerage firm is an open-end investment company (mutual fund) that purchases money market securities. These securities are short-term debt obligations with high liquidity. *Liquidity* means an investment may be converted to cash quickly and easily. Funds attempt to maintain the price of the fund at $1 per share. The price typically does not vary although the fund cannot guarantee that the price will not change. You normally earn dividends daily, and it may be paid to your account daily, weekly or monthly. The dividend yield may fluctuate based on the change in short-term interest rates and the securities held in the fund's portfolio.

Benefits of Money Market Funds

You may already use money market funds as part of your portfolio to provide liquidity, safety of principal and current income. They may be used as reserve accounts for your money while you decide where to invest next.

How Money Market Funds Are Classified

Money market funds offer either taxable or tax-free dividends, depending on the underlying securities held in the portfolio.

Taxable Money Market Funds. *Regular* money market funds invest in short-term securities, such as U.S. Treasury bills and notes, commercial paper and certificates of deposit (CDs). *Government* money market funds typically invest in U.S. Treasury and federal agency securities.

Tax-Free Money Market Funds. *Municipal* money market funds invest in short-term municipal notes. The dividends received are exempt from federal income taxation.

Brokerage Firms' Money Market Funds

Most brokerage firms' money market funds are not insured; however, their safety as investments for preservation of principal is potentially high. Some brokerage firms do offer insured money market accounts. If your objective is safety of principal, consider investing a portion of your assets in an insured money market account.

Bank Money Market Deposit Accounts

A *money market deposit account* (MMDA) offered by a bank or savings institution is not the same as a money market fund offered by a brokerage firm. Specifically, the yields and your ability to make withdrawals from the money market account differ. Money market accounts are insured by the FDIC. Before investing in either a money market fund or a money market account, compare the differences between them, the rates of return, liquidity and safety of each.

Your Portfolio Investment Questions (PIQs)

Money market funds and money market deposit accounts are fairly easy to grasp. Following are a few PIQs to help you get the most out of your choices.

 INVESTOR'S TIPS

- Money market funds and money market deposit accounts are investments for a portion of your *serious money*.
- You can use money market funds and money market deposit accounts for two purposes: (1) as *reserve accounts,* where you can collect income, deposits and proceeds from sales of securities while you wait to make new investments and (2) as *income-producing funds with safety of principal,* where you can keep some of your serious money.

Mastering Money Market Funds

Your Portfolio Investment Questions (PIQs)

Name of investment _____ **Date** _____

1. How may I obtain a current prospectus, annual report and other information?

   Name _____

   Firm _____

   Address _____ Telephone number _____

   _____ Fax number _____

2. Is this a money market fund or a money market deposit account?

   _____ Money market fund

   _____ Money market deposit account

3. If it is a money market fund, what is the classification?

   _____ Regular   _____ Insured   _____ Municipal

   _____ Government   _____ Other _____

4. If it is a money market fund, what are some of the underlying securities?

5. If it is a money market fund, who is the custodian for the shares?

6. If it is a money market fund, what is the insurance coverage?

7. If it is a money market deposit account, what is the insurance coverage?

8. How often can I withdraw funds?

✏ Mastering Money Market Funds (Continued)

Your Portfolio Investment Questions (PIQs)

Name of investment _____ **Date** _____

9. How long does it take to receive the withdrawal?

10. Are checkwriting privileges provided? _____ Yes _____ No
    If so, what are the restrictions?

11. What is the current yield?

12. Are the dividends I receive taxable or tax exempt?

13. Are statements issued? If so, how often?

Notes

CHAPTER 10

Comparing Certificates of Deposit (CDs)

More than $1 trillion are invested in large and small time deposits, commonly known as certificates of deposit (CDs), as reported by the Federal Reserve Bank of St. Louis. *Certificates of deposit* are issued by commercial banks, savings banks and savings and loan associations. CDs are normally issued in denominations of $1,000 and pay interest monthly, quarterly, semiannually or annually. The interest earned is federally taxable, and the principal is insured by the Federal Deposit Insurance Corporation (FDIC), a governmental agency. Each depositor's funds are insured by the FDIC up to $100,000. For a more comprehensive explanation of the FDIC, contact the Federal Deposit Insurance Corporation. See Appendix C, "Resources," for the address.

The Truth-in-Savings Act created a standard method for calculating the *annual percentage yield* (APY) on a CD. Therefore, each financial institution must state the APY so you may compare one interest rate to another.

Benefits of CDs

CDs offer safety of principal, liquidity and current income. They are an investment for a portion of your serious money—that is, money you do not want to risk losing.

Maturity Dates

CDs have different maturity dates, usually ranging from one week to ten years. The interest rate offered depends on the maturity. A concept that has been used in recent years is to "ladder" CDs. See Financial Focus 4 for a further explanation of laddering CDs, as well as other securities.

Brokerage Firm CDs

Brokerage firms offer CDs issued by banks and thrifts across the country. The CDs are FDIC insured and physical certificates are not issued. These CDs are usually negotiable, so you can sell one in a secondary CD market before the maturity date. The amount you receive may be more or less than what you invested, depending on the change in interest rates. Of course, if you hold the CD to maturity, you will receive the full amount invested plus interest. The interest is paid to you or credited to your brokerage account, rather than reinvested in the CD.

Bank CDs

Banks offer only CDs they issue themselves. The CDs are FDIC insured, and certificates may or may not be issued. These CDs are usually not negotiable but may be redeemed before the maturity dates. The amount you receive will be the same as what you invested, but you will pay a penalty on the interest. Of course, if you hold a CD to maturity, you will earn the full amount invested plus interest. The interest may be paid to you, credited to one of your other accounts or reinvested in the CD.

Your Portfolio Investment Questions (PIQs)

CDs have been a popular investment tool, but you have to shop around for the best rate. The following PIQs may help you select the appropriate ones in establishing a CD ladder portfolio. Ask your investment professional or banker these PIQs so that you can understand better the terms of the CD.

 INVESTOR'S TIPS

- CDs are an investment for a portion of your *serious money*.
- *Laddering CDs* for a portion of your portfolio is a *good strategy*.
- Because the rate of return from CDs varies among financial institutions, you may want to shop around for the best rate.
- Yields on CDs may be competitive with other fixed-income securities.

Comparing Certificates of Deposit (CDs)

Your Portfolio Investment Questions (PIQs)

Name of investment _____ **Date** _____

1. Who issues the CD, and what area does the issuer serve?

2. What is the maturity date?

3. What is the annual percentage yield (APY)?

4. How often and when is the interest paid?

5. What is the cost to purchase the CD?

6. What is the cost or penalty to liquidate the CD prior to maturity?

7. Will a certificate be issued to me in my name, held in street name in my brokerage account or held in my bank account?

Notes

CHAPTER 11

Comprehending Fixed Annuities

A *fixed annuity* is a contract between an insurance company and an individual. A fixed annuity contract has at least four entities: (1) issuer, (2) owner, (3) annuitant and (4) beneficiary. An *annuity* is a contract that the issuer (the insurance company) will pay the annuitant (the recipient of the distributions) a specified amount for a specified time when the annuity is annuitized, based on the contract terms. The *accumulation* period is from the time an annuity is purchased to when the annuity is annuitized. *Annuitize* means that the annuity begins to pay income and principal to the annuitant.

A fixed annuity is only one kind of annuity. We will discuss variable annuities and immediate annuities in the next two chapters.

Nonqualified Annuities

Two broad categories of annuities are *qualified* and *nonqualified*. The terms refer to whether the annuity is part of an employee retirement plan. A *qualified annuity* is used in a retirement plan that meets certain requirements under the Internal Revenue Code. A *nonqualified annuity* is not used as part of a qualified retirement plan. This discussion of annuities in this book refers only to nonqualified annuities.

Benefits of a Tax-Deferred Fixed Annuity

The benefits of owning a tax-deferred fixed annuity are (1) the principal guarantee, (2) the income guarantee and (3) the tax-deferred income (if eligible under the Internal Revenue Code). Fixed annuities are not normally purchased to provide current income, although partial withdrawals may be made. The objective is to let the annuity earn tax-deferred interest and accumulate until you decide to surrender the contract or annuitize it.

The Key Parties to Annuities

An *insurance company* issues annuities. The company promises to invest your premium prudently, credit interest to your funds purchased in your annuity, pay the beneficiary the death benefit in the event of your death if prior to annuitization and make payments to you according to your selected settlement option.

The *owner* is the individual who purchases the annuity and may change the beneficiary or other elements of the annuity. The owner may also liquidate or annuitize the annuity.

The *annuitant* can be the person who receives payment when the annuity is annuitized or the person whose age is used to calculate payments to the beneficiary if the owner dies. In many cases, the owner and the annuitant are the same individual.

The *beneficiary* generally is the individual or entity who receives the death benefit of the annuity if the owner, and in some cases, the annuitant dies before the annuity is annuitized. When the beneficiary is a surviving spouse, the payment of the death benefit may be altered so that the annuity remains in force with the surviving spouse as the new owner.

Guarantees of a Fixed Annuity

The insurance company guarantees both the principal, excluding surrender charges and any market value adjustments, and interest based on the terms of the contract. The interest earned may vary over time depending on the insurance company's earnings and what rate the contract guarantees.

Features of a Tax-Deferred Fixed Annuity

A tax-deferred fixed annuity is a common policy offered by insurance companies directly or through other financial service firms. Typically, the contract provides a guaranteed payment of principal minus any sales charges upon surrender (liquidation). Generally, a fixed annuity contract offers two interest rates: (1) a guaranteed rate; and (2) a current interest rate. The guaranteed rate is the lowest rate that will be credited to your funds regardless of the current interest rate. The current interest rate is the rate that the insurance company may credit your funds based upon the earnings of the company. However, the current interest rate may be guaranteed for one year or longer. After the initial term has ended, a new interest rate is usually guaranteed annually. Fixed annuities share some characteristics of other fixed income investments, with the following exceptions: (1) The annuity is issued by an insurance company; (2) interest on the annuity is tax deferred; and (3) the annuity's principal is guaranteed by the insurance company.

Income Payment Options

The owner may select to receive the annuity's benefits or may annuitize it based on several different income payment options, such as (1) life income, (2) period certain, (3) life with period certain and (4) joint and survivor. Other payment options may also be available. Income payment options are also known as *settlement options* or *benefit options.*

Life Income. The life income payment option pays the annuitant (or other designated beneficiary) a guaranteed income *for life.* When the annuitant dies, the income payments stop. Under this option, you hope you live a long time (of course, you hope to live a long time in any case). The insurance company benefits if the annuitant lives less time than it expects because the company keeps any unpaid balance.

Period Certain. The period certain income payment option pays the annuitant (or other designated beneficiary) a guaranteed income *for a certain period of time.* If the annuitant dies before the period ends, the insurance company pays the beneficiary the same payment for the remaining number of years in the term. For example, if the period is ten years and the annuitant dies in the eighth year, the beneficiary receives the same payment for two more years. However, if the annuitant receives payments for ten years and later dies, the beneficiary receives no payments.

Life with Period Certain. The life with period certain income payment option pays the annuitant (or other designated beneficiary) a guaranteed income *for life* or pays another individual the same payment for a certain number of years. For example, if the period is ten years and the annuitant dies in the eighth year, the beneficiary receives the same payment for two more years. However, if the annuitant receives payments for ten years and then dies, the beneficiary receives no payments.

Joint and Survivor. The joint and survivor income payment option pays two annuitants a guaranteed income *for both lives.* If one annuitant dies, the payment continues until the second annuitant dies. The insurance company makes no payments after the second individual dies.

The Cost of Buying Fixed Annuities

Annuities may be purchased with a single payment or with payments over a stated period of time. Annuities are usually sold without an up-front sales charge, although the insurance agent normally receives a commission advanced by the insurance company. The company will also deduct operating expenses annually from the annuity contract. Upon liquidation, you may pay a surrender charge. Annuity contracts may differ on the amount of surrender charge and how many years must elapse before no charge applies. Many annuities have a declining sales charge over a five-year to ten-year period. However, if you annuitize the contract, surrender charges are usually waived.

Interest and Taxation

If the annuity contract meets certain conditions of the Internal Revenue Code, then the interest earned and reinvested in the annuity is not taxed. However, when the interest is paid to you, it is taxed as ordinary income—hence, the name *tax-deferred annuity*. If principal is paid to you, you incur no income tax.

If you partially withdraw money from the annuity, the withdrawal is considered taxable income until all of the interest earned in the annuity is paid out. Subsequent withdrawals are considered principal and are not taxed.

Fixed annuities have special tax provisions regarding withdrawals for persons younger than age 59½. In such a case, the interest withdrawn is subject to a 10 percent penalty tax in addition to the income tax. Withdrawals after age 59½ do not incur a 10 percent penalty tax.

How Are Insurance Companies Rated?

A.M. Best Company, Duff & Phelps Credit Rating Company, Moody's Investors Service and Standard & Poor's Insurance Ratings Services are independent agencies that rate insurance companies based on their financial strengths and ability to perform the annuity contract. Consider these ratings when you purchase an annuity.

Following are the ratings used by A.M. Best Company:

Rating	Definition
Secure Ratings	
A++	Superior
A+	Superior
A	Excellent
A–	Excellent
B++	Very good
B+	Very good

Rating	Definition
Vulnerable Ratings	
B	Adequate
B–	Adequate
C++	Fair
C+	Fair
C	Marginal
C–	Marginal

Consult the rating service for expanded definitions for each rating category. See Appendix C, "Resources," for the address.

Your Portfolio Investment Questions (PIQs)

Though fixed annuities may seem fairly straightforward, you need to understand a few items—such as renewal rates, sales charges and surrender charges—before you invest. Since numerous insurance companies offer fixed annuities, ask your insurance professional for several alternatives. Use the following PIQs to help you understand fixed annuities so you may select a suitable annuity.

 ## INVESTOR'S TIPS

- Consider fixed annuities as an investment for a portion of your *serious money.*
- Compounding tax-deferred interest is *powerful.*
- *Read the policy* carefully regarding all sales costs and surrender charges.
- Understand how the interest rates are *renewed.*

Comprehending Fixed Annuities

Your Portfolio Investment Questions (PIQs)

Name of investment _____ Date _____

1. How may I obtain a sample policy, research report and/or ratings report?

   Name _____

   Firm _____

   Address _____ Telephone number _____

   _____ Fax number   _____

2. Who issues the fixed annuity?

3. What is the *A.M. Best* rating for the insurance company? (Check one.)

   _____ A++   _____ A–   _____ B

   _____ A+   _____ B++   _____ B–

   _____ A   _____ B+   _____ Other _____

4. What is the initial interest rate?

5. How long is the initial interest rate guaranteed?

6. How long is the renewal rate guaranteed?

7. What has been the issuer's renewal rate history?

8. What is the death benefit?

Comprehending Fixed Annuities   (Continued)

Your Portfolio Investment Questions (PIQs)

Name of investment _____ **Date** _____

9. What are the sales charges or fees for buying the fixed annuity?

10. What are the sales charges or fees for surrendering (liquidating) the fixed annuity?

11. What are the income payment options if I annuitize?

    _____ Life income   _____ Joint and survivor

    _____ Period certain   _____ Other _____

    _____ Life with period certain

12. What is my potential gain from purchasing the fixed annuity?

13. What is my potential loss from purchasing the fixed annuity?

Notes

CHAPTER 12

Learning about Variable Annuities

A *variable annuity* (VA) is a contract between an insurance company and an individual. A *tax-deferred variable annuity* is a contract offered by insurance companies directly or through other financial service firms. A variable annuity contract has at least four entities: (1) issuer, (2) owner, (3) annuitant (4) and beneficiary. An *annuity* is a contract that the issuer (the insurance company) will pay the annuitant (the recipient of the distributions) a specified amount for a specified time when the annuity is annuitized based on the contract terms. The accumulation period is from the time an annuity is purchased to when the annuity is annuitized. *Annuitize* means that the annuity begins to pay income and principal to the annuitant. Variable annuities are risk-oriented investments.

Benefits of a Tax-Deferred Variable Annuity

The benefit of owning a tax-deferred variable annuity is the potential for above-average returns because your assets may be invested in the securities markets and assume actual risk. If the annuity contract meets certain conditions of the Internal Revenue Code, then the earnings, if left in the variable annuity, are not taxed. Variable annuities are not normally purchased to provide current income, although partial withdrawals may be made. The objective is to let the annuity increase in value and accumulate tax deferred until you surrender the contract or annuitize it. Over the course of time, you may receive varying rates of returns depending on your selection of the investment accounts and performance by the insurance company. You may select the investment category among accounts, such as stock account, bond account and guaranteed account. Each variable annuity may offer you various types of accounts with different types of investment objectives. The guaranteed account provides you with a fixed rate of interest for a certain time period, whereas the other investment accounts provide you with a "variable" return depending on the risk and performance of the particular investment selection.

Since a variable annuity is a security, a prospectus must be given to you with or preceding a specific proposal. The prospectus provides information about the investment choices, risks and the variable annuity.

The Key Parties to Annuities

An *insurance company* issues annuities. The company promises to invest your premium prudently, credit interest to your funds purchased in your annuity, pay the beneficiary the death benefit in the event of your death (if your death is prior to annuitization) and make payments to you according to your selected settlement option.

The *owner* is the individual who purchases the annuity and may change the beneficiary or other elements of the annuity. The owner may also liquidate the annuity.

The *annuitant* can be the person who receives payment when the annuity is annuitized or the person whose age is used to calculate payments to the beneficiary if the owner dies. In many cases, the owner and the annuitant are the same individual.

The *beneficiary* generally is the individual or entity who receives the annuity's death benefit if the owner, and in some cases, the annuitant dies before the annuity is annuitized. When the beneficiary is a surviving spouse, the death benefit payment may be altered so that the annuity remains in force with the surviving spouse as the new owner.

Guarantees of a Variable Annuity

The insurance company *does not guarantee* either the principal or the rate of return for a variable annuity, as it does for a fixed annuity. The rate of return will vary over time depending on the performance of the assets in the variable annuity. Some variable annuities offer a death benefit based on the original investment or the valuation on the policy's anniversary date. This feature helps the beneficiary because the contract's market value always changes.

Features of a Variable Annuity

Typically, the variable annuity contract provides you with an opportunity to invest in securities, such as bonds, stocks, money market securities and others. You may allocate your investments among several asset categories depending on the outlook of the various markets. Some variable annuities offer a fixed rate account, in which the interest rate return is set for one year. Usually, you may exchange your funds in one investment category for funds in another without any sales charge. Buying variable annuities has some similarities with buying mutual funds, but under the structure of annuities. (Mutual funds will be discussed in Chapter 18.)

The valuation of your investment accounts is represented by the net asset value (NAV). The NAV is the price of the investment account. Your total return is determined by the performance of each investment account. A prospectus is available along with the annuity contract, which explains the investment objective of each investment category and all the sales charges and expenses.

Income Payment Options

You may liquidate the annuity or annuitize it based on several income payment options, such as (1) life income, (2) period certain, (3) life with period certain and (4) joint and survivor. See Chapter 11 for details on these payment options.

Cost of Buying a Variable Annuity

You may purchase an annuity with a single payment or with payments over a period of time. Annuities are usually sold without an upfront sales charge, although the insurance agent normally receives a commission advanced by the insurance company. The company will also deduct operating expenses annually from the annuity contract. Upon liquidation, you might pay a surrender charge. Annuity contracts may differ depending on the amount of surrender charge and how many years must elapse before there is no charge. Many annuities have a declining sales charge over a five-year to ten-year period. However, if you annuitize the contract, the surrender charge is usually waived.

Interest and Taxation

If the annuity contract meets certain conditions of the Internal Revenue Code, then the earnings, if left in the variable annuity, are not taxed. However, when the earnings are paid to you, they are taxed as ordinary income—hence, the name *tax-deferred annuity*. If you receive the principal, you incur no income tax.

If you partially withdraw money from the annuity, the withdrawal is considered taxable income until all of the earnings in the annuity are paid out. Subsequent withdrawals are considered principal and are not taxed.

Variable annuities have a special tax provision regarding withdrawals for persons younger than age 59½. The earnings they withdraw are subject to a 10 percent penalty tax in addition to the income tax. Withdrawals after a person reaches age 59½ do not incur a 10 percent penalty tax. Check with your certified public accountant or tax attorney for a comprehensive explanation of taxation for annuities.

How Are Insurance Companies Rated?

A.M. Best Company, Duff & Phelps Credit Rating Company, Moody's Investors Service and Standard & Poor's Insurance Ratings Services are independent agencies that rate insurance companies based on their financial strengths and ability to perform the annuity contract.

Consider these ratings when you purchase an annuity. See Chapter 11 for more information on ratings.

Your Portfolio Investment Questions (PIQs)

Ask your insurance professional for information and a prospectus for several variable annuities. When buying variable annuities, you may select different types of investments. A particular investment offers both risk and reward; therefore, the following PIQs may help you match the appropriate variable annuity investment to your investment objective.

 INVESTOR'S TIPS

- Variable annuities are an investment for a portion of your *investment money.*
- Compounding tax-deferred interest and capital gains is *powerful* for accumulating assets.
- Read the *full prospectus* and *policy* carefully, and *focus on the following:*
  - Fund's investment objective
  - Risk factors
  - Types of investments that may be purchased in the investment account
  - Allocation of assets within the investment accounts
  - Current and past investment income
  - Distribution rate
  - Past performance (total return) of the investment accounts
  - Sales charges, surrender charges and expenses
  - Investment manager's credentials

Learning about Variable Annuities

Your Portfolio Investment Questions (PIQs)

Name of investment _____ **Date** _____

1. How may I obtain a prospectus, sample policy, research report and/or ratings report?

   Name _____

   Firm _____

   Address _____ Telephone number _____

   _____ Fax number   _____

2. Who issues the variable annuity?

3. What is the *A.M. Best* rating for the insurance company? (Check one.)

   _____ A++   _____ A−   _____ B

   _____ A+   _____ B++   _____ B−

   _____ A   _____ B+   _____ Other _____

4. What is my investment objective?

   _____ Growth   _____ Income

   _____ Long-term growth   _____ Preservation of capital

   _____ Growth and income

5. What has been the past performance of each investment account?

6. How is the death benefit calculated?

7. What are the sales charges or fees for buying the variable annuity?

🖉 Learning about Variable Annuities (Continued)

Your Portfolio Investment Questions (PIQs)

Name of investment _____ **Date** _____

8. What are the sales charges or fees for surrendering (liquidating) the variable annuity?

9. What are the income payment options if I annuitize?

    _____ Life income   _____ Joint and survivor

    _____ Period certain   _____ Other _____

    _____ Life with period certain

10. What kind of investments will the insurance company purchase for each investment account?

11. What economic scenario could cause the value of the selected investment account to increase?

12. What is my potential gain from purchasing the variable annuity?

13. What economic scenario could cause the value of the selected investment account to decrease?

14. What is my potential loss from purchasing the variable annuity?

Notes

CHAPTER 13

Living with Immediate Annuities

An *immediate annuity* is a contract between an insurance company and an individual. It is a common policy offered by insurance companies directly or through other financial service firms. The immediate annuity contract has at least four entities: (1) issuer, (2) owner, (3) annuitant and (4) owner's beneficiary. An *annuity* is a contract that states that the issuer (the insurance company) will pay the annuitant (the recipient of the distributions) a specified amount for a specified time when the annuity is annuitized based on the contract terms. *Annuitize* means that the annuity begins to pay income and principal to the annuitant.

Benefit of an Immediate Annuity

The benefit of owning an immediate annuity is the guaranteed payment of both principal and income to you over the selected payment option period. Immediate annuities are normally purchased to provide cash flow for your lifetime or over a period of time.

The Key Parties to Annuities

An *insurance company* issues annuities. The company promises to invest your premium prudently and make payments to you or your beneficiary according to your selected income payment option.

The *owner* is the individual who purchases the annuity and may change the beneficiary.

The *annuitant* can be the person who receives the payment when the annuity is annuitized, or the person whose age is used to calculate payments to the annuitant. In many cases, the owner and the annuitant are the same individual.

The owner's *beneficiary* generally is the individual who receives the death benefit of the annuity if the owner dies prior to the annuity starting date or becomes the owner upon the death of the owner(s) on or after the annuity starting date. The benefit depends on the selected income payment options.

Guarantees of an Immediate Annuity

The insurance company guarantees the payment based on the contract terms. The payment typically will not vary over time once the annuity is annuitized.

Features of an Immediate Annuity

Usually, the contract provides you with a guaranteed payment. Annuity payments usually begin one month after you purchase an annuity–hence, the name *immediate annuity*. Payments can be made monthly, quarterly, semiannually or annually.

Income Payment Options

You may annuitize the annuity based on several income payment options, such as (1) life income, (2) period certain, (3) life with period certain and (4) joint and survivor. See Chapter 11 for details on these payment options.

The Cost of Buying an Immediate Annuity

You may purchase an immediate annuity with a single payment. They are usually sold without an up-front sales charge, although the insurance agent normally receives a commission advanced by the insurance company. The company will also deduct operating expenses annually from the annuity contract.

Interest and Taxation

Because each payment you receive is part income and part return of principal, only the income portion is taxed as ordinary income. The insurance company will calculate the *exclusion ratio*—the percentage portion of your payment (return of principal) that is *not* taxed as ordinary income. Check with your certified public accountant or tax attorney for a comprehensive explanation of taxation for annuities.

How Are Insurance Companies Rated?

A.M. Best Company, Duff & Phelps Credit Rating Company, Moody's Investors Service and Standard & Poor's Insurance Ratings Services are independent agencies that rate insurance companies based on their financial strengths and ability to perform the annuity contract. Consider these ratings when you purchase an annuity. See Chapter 11 for more information on ratings.

Your Portfolio Investment Questions (PIQs)

You purchase an immediate annuity to receive the guaranteed payment of interest and principal. Ask your insurance professional to discuss the suitability of immediate annuities for you. Therefore, ask the appropriate PIQs so that you know when and for how long you will receive your payments.

 INVESTOR'S TIPS

- Immediate annuities are the investment for you if you want to receive *guaranteed regularly scheduled income.*
- The payment you receive consists of *both* principal and interest.
- *Read the policy* carefully regarding all sales costs and expenses.
- Understand the income payment option you select.

Living with Immediate Annuities

Your Portfolio Investment Questions (PIQs)

Name of investment _____ **Date** _____

1. How may I obtain a sample policy, research report or ratings report?

    Name   _____

    Firm   _____

    Address _____ Telephone number _____

    _____ Fax number _____

2. Who issues the immediate annuity?

3. What is the *A.M. Best* rating for the insurance company? (Check one.)

    _____ A++   _____ A−   _____ B

    _____ A+   _____ B++   _____ B−

    _____ A   _____ B+   _____ Other _____

4. What are the income payment options when I annuitize?

    _____ Life income   _____ Period certain

    _____ Life with period certain _____ Joint and survivor

    _____ Other _____

5. When will the payments be made?

6. What is the payment amount?

7. What is the exclusion ratio?

8. What are the sales charges or fees for buying the immediate annuity?

✎ Living with Immediate Annuities (Continued)

Your Portfolio Investment Questions (PIQs)

Name of investment _____ Date _____

9. What economic scenario could cause the amount of payment from the immediate annuity to increase?

10. What is my potential gain from purchasing the immediate annuity?

11. What economic scenario could cause the amount of payment from the immediate annuity to decrease?

12. What is my potential loss from purchasing the immediate annuity?

Notes

CHAPTER 14

Making Use of Life Insurance

Why buy life insurance nowadays if the average life expectancy for men and women exceeds age 75?

The future is unknown, and people need to plan for the unexpected. Life insurance helps you fulfill this objective by providing a monetary payment to your beneficiaries upon your death. A *life insurance policy* is a contract between an insurance company and an individual and involves at least four parties: (1) insurer, (2) owner, (3) insured and (4) beneficiary. The policy (purchased by the owner) guarantees that the insurer (the insurance company) will pay the beneficiary (the recipient of the proceeds) a specified amount (the death benefit) when the insured dies.

Benefits of Buying Life Insurance

Proceeds from a life insurance policy may provide money for (1) funeral expenses, (2) inheritance taxes, (3) creation of an estate, (4) financial support of the surviving family, (5) business purposes,

(6) financial assistance to your heirs and many other purposes. Furthermore, many life insurance policies accumulate sufficient cash value and serve as income-producing assets when they are paid up.

Components of an Insurance Policy

All insurance policies have at least four components: (1) mortality expense, (2) commissions, (3) operating expense and (4) cash value. *Mortality expense* covers the pure insurance part of the policy. *Commissions (loading expense)* are paid to the insurance agent, while *operating expenses* are deducted by the insurance company.

Cash value is the accumulated earnings of the policy, if any, after all expenses and commissions are paid. If you cancel the policy, you receive the cash surrender value, which is the cash value less any sales charges. Additionally, you may borrow your cash value based on the contract terms. The insurance company may charge you interest on your policy loan.

Policy Illustration

Your insurance agent should provide you with an illustration showing the guaranteed cash value, estimated cash value, cash surrender value and death benefit for each year of the policy. The table should also state the guaranteed interest rate, the current market interest rate and the scheduled premiums.

Types of Policies

Insurance companies issue many variations of life insurance policies. Four basic types of policies are (1) term, (2) permanent, (3) universal and (4) variable.

Term. Term life insurance provides a death benefit for a limited period of time, such as 1, 5, 10 or 20 years. After the specified time, insurance coverage ceases. The premiums paid do not accumulate as cash value and pay for only the insurance and policy expenses. Although term insurance is normally the least expensive type of insurance, you get more death benefit per dollar than with other types of policies.

Permanent. Sometimes referred to as *whole life,* permanent life insurance provides a death benefit for the life of the insured. The insurance premiums must be paid throughout the insured's life, or at least until age 100. If the insured lives to age 100, the policy is paid up with the cash values equaling the face amount of the policy. Permanent life insurance may be issued as a *participating policy,* which offers the opportunity for dividends to (1) reduce premiums, (2) purchase paid-up additions (i.e., increase the death benefit) and (3) increase cash value by accumulating interest. You may withdraw the cash value by borrowing from the policy. The insurance company may charge you interest on the loan. If you cancel the policy, the insurance company pays you the *cash surrender value,* which is the cash value less any charges and loans outstanding.

Universal. Universal life insurance is a form of whole life with the ability to change two features of the policy. Over the course of the policy, you may adjust the death benefit and make flexible premium payments based upon the contract terms. Generally, under permanent life and term insurance, the death benefit and premiums cannot be changed. Most policies pay an interest rate competitive to money market interest rates. The current interest rate may change over the life of the policy and is not guaranteed. The guaranteed interest rate is usually low and may not be able to sustain the policy without additional premiums being paid. The amount of premiums you pay, the mortality expenses and the earnings from the cash value normally determine the death benefit. *Single premium universal life* policies are offered in which you pay only one premium payment.

Variable. Variable life insurance is similar to universal life, except that the cash value can be invested in a portfolio of stocks and bonds. Your cash value and death benefit may fluctuate in value depending upon the performance of the underlying portfolio. Since variable life insurance is a security, a prospectus must be delivered to you with or preceding a specific proposal.

In-Force Illustration

Once you have purchased a life insurance policy, ask your agent annually for an *in-force policy illustration,* also known as a *point-in-time illustration.* An in-force policy illustration contains at least a table showing you guaranteed cash values, estimated cash values, cash surrender values and death benefit for the remaining years of the policy. These figures provide you with an update of how well your estimated cash values and/or death benefits are doing relative to the original projections. If the values do not keep pace with the original projections, discuss with your insurance agent the reasons for the differences.

How Are Life Insurance Companies Rated?

A.M. Best Company, Duff & Phelps Credit Rating Company, Moody's Investors Service and Standard & Poor's Insurance Ratings Services are independent agencies that rate insurance companies based on their financial strengths and ability to perform the life insurance contract. Consider these ratings when you purchase a life insurance policy. See Chapter 11 for more information on ratings.

Your Portfolio Investment Questions (PIQs)

Life insurance may not be the most comfortable topic to discuss, but it is a necessary and important part of your estate planning. Some life insurance can be complicated. Ask your insurance professional about the various types of insurance policies that may be suitable for you. However, asking a few PIQs can help you select the best policy for your financial and estate planning needs.

INVESTOR'S TIPS

- Life insurance is an *integral part* of your *financial* and *estate planning.*
- Life insurance may be used for medical and funeral expenses, children's education and *the financial welfare of your loved ones.*
- *Read the policy* carefully regarding all *sales costs, expenses* and *surrender charges.*
- Understand the guaranteed interest rate and current interest rate.
- Review your policy periodically by asking for an in-force illustration, especially if your circumstances and goals change (e.g., you marry, have children, etc.).

Making Use of Life Insurance

Your Portfolio Investment Questions (PIQs)

Name of investment _____ **Date** _____

1. How may I obtain a sample policy, research report or ratings report?

   Name _____

   Firm _____

   Address _____ Telephone number _____

   _____ Fax number   _____

2. Are you an independent insurance agent? _____ Yes _____ No

3. If so, what companies do you represent?

4. Who issues the life insurance policy?

5. What is the *A.M. Best* rating for the insurance company? (Check one.)

   _____ A++   _____ A−   _____ B

   _____ A+   _____ B++   _____ B−

   _____ A   _____ B+   _____ Other _____

6. What type of policy is it? (Check one.)

   _____ Term life   _____ Permanent life

   _____ Universal life   _____ Variable life   _____ Other _____

7. What is the death benefit?

8. Is the premium single payment or periodic payment?

9. If single, how much is the premium?

Making Use of Life Insurance (Continued)

Your Portfolio Investment Questions (PIQs)

Name of investment _____ Date _____

10. If periodic, how much is the premium? How often is the premium due?

11. What is the guaranteed interest rate?

12. What is the current interest rate?

13. May I have an illustration of the amount of death benefit, guaranteed values, projected accumulated values and cash surrender values for the life of the policy?

14. What are the costs if I cancel the policy?

15. If I have a term policy, can I convert it to a permanent life policy?

16. What are the income payment options if I surrender the policy?

17. What economic scenario could cause the premium payment to increase?

18. What economic scenario could cause the premium payment to decrease?

Notes

CHAPTER 15

Buying Bonds, Notes and Bills

Ten trillion dollars is the approximate size of the corporate, government and municipal debt markets. *Bonds, notes* and *bills* are debt obligations of the issuer. Also called *debt* or *debt securities,* bonds are issued by the U.S. government, federal agencies, corporations and municipalities, such as states, counties, cities or any political subdivision thereof. The *issuer* is the debtor and is obligated to pay the bondholder (creditor) interest and principal at maturity.

Benefits of Buying Bonds, Notes and Bills

The primary benefit of buying bonds, notes and bills is the interest income you can receive. Your principal is secure if you hold the bond, note or bill to maturity, assuming the issuer has the financial means to pay the debt at maturity.

Features of Debt Securities

Par value is typically $1,000 and is also known as the *face value* or *principal amount.* The price of the debt security is normally quoted as a percent of par value. At maturity, the holder receives the par value of the security. One point is equal to $10 when quoting a debt security. For example, a quote of 100 represents $1,000, a quote of 90¼ represents $902.50 and a quote of 101.50 represents $1,010.50.

Interest is paid based on the coupon rate of the bond, which is generally fixed and set at issuance. The *coupon rate* is the interest rate stated on the debt security representing the amount of interest paid by the issuer on the principal of the issue. For example, a coupon rate of 8 percent (also called a *nominal yield*) pays the bondholder $80 per year per $1,000. Generally, bonds and notes pay interest semiannually, either on the 1st or 15th of the month. Zero-coupon bonds and notes are offered at a *discount* (less than $1,000 par value) and do not pay out any interest until maturity. Instead, interest accumulates until maturity at which time the holder receives $1,000. The difference between what you paid for the zero-coupon bond or note and $1,000 is the *accreted income.*

Interest received from government and corporate debt issues is federally taxed as income. However, interest from municipal debt issues is exempt from federal income taxation. Government and corporate zero-coupon bondholders typically must pay tax each year on the earned interest even though they did not receive income in that year. This is known as *phantom income.* Holders of zero-coupon municipal bonds typically do not have to pay tax on the earned interest each year. See Financial Focus 5 for a comparison of taxable yields and tax-exempt yields.

Bond issuers, primarily corporations, normally establish a provision, known as the *call provision,* in which they may redeem the bond prior to its maturity date. For instance, the bond issuer may buy back the bond after a certain date at a specified price, normally more than $1,000 per bond. The corporation may call a bond if it is able to issue a new bond at a lower interest cost than the issue being redeemed. Usually calling a bond works to the advantage of the corporation but not to the advantage of the bondholder whose bond is being redeemed.

Some bonds may be *convertible* into the common stock of the corporate issuer. The *conversion ratio* represents the number of shares and price per common share that the bond can be converted into. You should understand these terms before you make any conversion. Convertible bonds offer two benefits: (1) payment of income at a stated rate and (2) capital appreciation once converted, if the underlying stock increases.

Types of Debt Securities

The three major categories of debt securities are government, municipal and corporate.

Government Securities. Government securities usually fall into one of two categories: U.S. Treasury and federal agencies. The U.S. Treasury issues bonds, notes and bills. While bonds have maturities ranging from 10 to 30 years or more, notes have maturities ranging from one to ten years. U.S. Treasury bills (T-bills) have maturities of one year or less. *Federal agency securities* (also known as *government agency securities* or simply *agencies*) are issued by U.S. government-sponsored agencies, such as Federal Home Loan Bank (FHLB), Federal National Mortgage Association (FNMA), Federal Home Loan Mortgage Corporation (FHLMC) and Tennessee Valley Authority (TVA).

U.S. Treasury securities are not rated by the rating agencies. However, they are considered the highest quality of debt securities because both the payment of interest and principal is guaranteed by the full faith and credit of the U.S. government. Most issues of government agencies are not guaranteed by the U.S. government. Since the agencies are part of the federal government, they carry a "moral" obligation of the U.S. government and are considered second only to U.S. Treasury securities in terms of credit quality.

Government bonds and notes normally have a fixed maturity date and stated interest payment dates. However, some government bonds and notes are issued with a zero-coupon rate and issued at a discount from par value. U.S. Treasury bills are offered at a discount and do not provide any current income to investors.

Municipal Securities. Debt securities issued by municipalities, such as states, counties, cities or any political subdivision thereof are known as *tax-free bonds* or *notes.* The two basic classifications are general obligation (GO) and revenue bonds. Typically, the payment of interest and principal of a *GO* is secured by the full faith and credit and general taxing power of the issuer. The payment of interest and principal of a *revenue bond* is secured by the specifically pledged revenues of the underlying project. Revenues may be in the form of earnings of the project being financed, such as toll bridge charges, waterworks receipts or hospital fees. Other sources of revenue may come from pledged taxes or fees, which may be unrelated to the use of the bond proceeds, such as sales tax, gasoline tax or school tuition fees.

Corporate Securities. Most debt securities issued by corporations are known generally as *corporate bonds* or *notes.* Two of the more common types of corporate debt issues are first mortgage bonds and debenture bonds. Generally, the payment of interest and principal of *first mortgage bonds* is secured by the underlying collateral of the issue, such as the corporation's plant, equipment or land. The payment of interest and principal of *debenture bonds* have no such security and therefore are known as *unsecured bonds.* When choosing and holding corporate bonds, pay attention to factors important to the issuer, including sales revenues, earnings, debt coverage and the economic prosperity of the particular industry.

Cost of Trading Debt Securities

Brokers use either of two methods to charge you for buying or selling bonds, notes and bills. The first way is to charge you a commission or fee. Called a *net trade,* the second way is to include the sales charge in the price. All municipal bonds and most government and corporate bonds are traded net. Any bonds traded on the exchanges are executed with a commission.

Why Interest Rates Change

Some economic variables that cause interest rates to change are credit demands for money, inflation, unemployment, recession, economic expansion, political environment, Federal Reserve System (Fed) policies, change of tax laws and government spending. The Federal Reserve, the U.S. monetary agent, adjusts interest rates to try to control inflation and economic growth. Congress, the U.S. fiscal agent, controls taxes and government spending, which directly affect the growth of the U.S. economy.

Why Bond Prices Change

Bond prices change as interest rates fluctuate in the marketplace. It is important to know that *bond prices decrease as interest rates rise, and bond prices increase as interest rates fall.* See Financial Focus 6 for further explanation of why bond prices change.

When interest rates change, long-term bonds and notes normally fluctuate more than short-term bonds and notes. Therefore, the best time to buy long-term bonds may be when long-term interest rates are high and are expected to fall. The best time to buy short-term notes may be when short-term rates are low and are expected to rise. See Financial Focus 7 for an explanation of yield curves. Since it is difficult to predict interest rate changes, many investors choose to ladder the maturities of the bonds in their portfolios. See Financial Focus 4 for more on laddering securities. In addition, if you hold the bond or note to maturity and the issuer has enough cash in the case of corporate or municipal bonds and notes, you will receive par value ($1,000 per bond or note). Even if the bond or note fluctuates while you hold it, you will receive $1,000 per bond or note if you keep it until maturity.

Calculating Returns

Bonds provide several types of returns: (1) current yield, (2) yield to call and (3) yield to maturity. You should understand all three to know what rate of return you can expect over the life of the bond. See Financial Focus 1 and Chapter 3 for more on these yields.

How Bonds Are Rated

When you buy a bond, its credit rating should be one of your main considerations. Most bonds are rated by Moody's Investors Service (Moody's) and Standard & Poor's (S&P) based on the issuer's ability to pay interest and principal at maturity. U.S. Treasury and government agencies securities are not rated; most corporate and municipal debt securities are rated. Bonds rated as being investment grade have one of the four highest ratings. Bonds rated below this level are considered low quality and are sometimes referred to as "junk" bonds, which means that they carry more risk and more potential for volatility. Some municipal bonds and notes are insured by an insurance company, which generally earns them an Aaa or AAA rating by Moody's or S&P, respectively. Consider these ratings when you buy a bond or note.

Following are the ratings for municipal and corporate bonds by both services:

Moody's[1]	Definition	Standard & Poor's[2]
Aaa	Highest quality	AAA
Aa	High quality	AA
A	Good quality	A
Baa	Adequate quality	BBB
Ba	Speculative	BB
B	Speculative	B
Caa, Ca, C	Speculative	CCC, CC, C
NR	Not rated	NR
	Default	D

The ratings from Aa to B may be modified by a "1, 2 or 3."

The ratings from AA to CCC may be modified by a "+" or "–."

Consult *Standard & Poor's Bond Guide* and *Moody's Annual Bond Record* for expanded definitions for each rating category. See Appendix C, "Resources," for addresses.

[1]Reprinted by permission of Moody's Investors Service, Inc.
[2]Reprinted by permission of Standard & Poor's, a division of The McGraw-Hill Companies.

Typical Description of a U.S. Treasury Bond

In this chapter, we have discussed many terms and calculations. Below is an example of a description of a U.S. Treasury bond with the respective explanations:

10M U.S. Treasury bond 8.00% due 10/01/16
at 98, 8.16% CY, 8.10% YTM

Explanation:

10M	=	principal quantity ($10,000; "M" represents thousand)
U.S. Treasury bond	=	description of security and issuer (U.S. government)
8.00%	=	coupon rate or nominal yield; generally fixed and set at issuance (pays 8 percent of $1,000 annually, or $80 per year)
10/01/16	=	maturity date (principal is returned to bondholder)
04/01 and 10/01	=	interest payment dates (every six months)
98	=	quoted price of bond (98 percent of 1,000, or $980)
8.16%	=	current yield; coupon rate divided by purchase price ($80 divided by $980)
8.10%	=	yield to maturity (total return of bond if held to maturity date)

Your Portfolio Investment Questions (PIQs)

Some of the terminology may be difficult to understand when reading about bonds, notes and bills. However, most investors, especially retired people, will own bonds or notes for income purposes sometime during their lives. Understanding how bonds trade and the impact of changing interest rates is important to know when managing your portfolio. The following PIQs can help you discover some of the pertinent information.

INVESTOR'S TIPS

- Bonds and notes are investments for a portion of your *investment money.*
- Treasury bills are an investment for a portion of your *serious money.*
- Bonds, notes and bills are investments for *income* purposes, except for zero-coupon bonds, which do not pay any income until maturity.
- Knowing and understanding the rating of bonds and notes are important.
- *As interest rates fall, bond prices increase.*
- *As interest rates rise, bond prices decrease.*

Buying Bonds, Notes and Bills

Your Portfolio Investment Questions (PIQs)

Name of investment _____ **Date** _____

1. How may I obtain a current research report or annual report of the issuer?

   Name _____

   Firm _____

   Address _____ Telephone number _____

   _____ Fax number   _____

2. Who issues the debt security?

   _____ U.S. Treasury   _____ Federal agency

   _____ Municipality   _____ Corporation

3. Is the security insured? If so, by whom?

4. What is the bond's rating? (Check one for each rating service.)

Moody's	*S&P*
_____ Aaa	_____ AAA
_____ Aa	_____ AA
_____ A	_____ A
_____ Baa	_____ BBB
_____ Ba	_____ BB
_____ B	_____ B
_____ Caa, Ca, C	_____ CCC, CC, C
_____ NR	_____ NR
_____ Other _____	_____ D
	_____ Other _____

Buying Bonds, Notes and Bills (Continued)

Your Portfolio Investment Questions (PIQs)

Name of investment _____ Date _____

5. What is the quoted purchase or market price?

6. What is the coupon rate, and when is interest paid?

7. Is the interest income taxable or tax-exempt?

8. What is the current yield (CY)?

9. What is the maturity date?

10. What is the yield to maturity (YTM)?

11. What are the call or redemption provisions?

12. What is the yield to call (YTC)?

13. Are interest rates anticipated to rise or fall?

14. What could cause the price to decrease in value?

15. What could cause the price to increase in value?

16. What are the bond's or note's strong and weak points?

17. Will the bond, note or bill be issued in certificate form to me or held in street name in my brokerage account?

CHAPTER 16

Selecting Common Stock

More than 2,570 companies from around the world list their shares on the New York Stock Exchange, according to the *NYSE 1994 Fact Book*. About 51 million Americans own stock in companies or shares in stock mutual funds. Like these millions of investors, you may want to include some common stock in your investment portfolio. More volatile than most bonds, common stock can give you long-term investment growth. In fact, historically, common stock has given investors the best return over a long period of time compared to CDs and U.S. Treasury bills and bonds. Each weekday, the evening news reports how the stock market performed, reflecting the market's importance to the public.

Benefits of Common Stock

The benefits of owning common stock are capital appreciation of investment and current income. On the other side, not all common stock pays income, and even stock that does may eventually reduce the amount or eliminate the income totally. Also, the volatility of stock may cause your investment to be unprofitable for you.

What Is Common Stock?

Corporations raise money (capital) to build plants, purchase equipment and expand their business by issuing shares of common stock. As an asset class, stocks are also known as equities. *Common stock* is an *equity* security because it represents ownership of the corporation. Capitalization equals the number of shares of stock multiplied by the share price. A stock certificate is issued to identify the shareholder. Common stock shareholders may vote upon mergers, recapitalization, election of board of directors, etc. They may also receive cash dividends or stock dividends if the board of directors declares them. See Financial Focus 8 for an explanation of cash dividend dates.

Trading Stock

Shares of stock are traded (bought and sold) on stock exchanges, such as the New York Stock Exchange (NYSE), American Stock Exchange (AMEX) and Pacific Stock Exchange (PSE), or in the Nasdaq Stock Market[SM]. Other securities not listed on the exchanges or in the Nasdaq market trade over-the-counter (OTC). The exchanges, Nasdaq and OTC market are secondary markets where investors buy and sell stocks with other investors, not with the companies.

Prices and Commissions

You will find stock quotations listed in the newspapers under their appropriate marketplaces. Throughout the day, the typical price variation of a stock is known as a *tick*, ⅛ of a dollar, or $.125, per share. In stock quotes, one point equals $1. For example, if you buy 100 shares of a stock priced at 39⅜, you would pay $3,937.50 (100 × 39.375) plus the commissions that stockbrokers charge when they place a buy or sell order for you.

Stock prices are quoted with a *bid price* and an *offer price.* The offer price is also known as the *asked price.* The bid price is the highest price that a buyer will pay for the stock; the offer price is the lowest price that a seller will take for the stock. Therefore, when you sell shares, you receive the bid price; when you buy shares, you pay the offer price. A share could be quoted like this: 58 (bid) – 58¼ (offer). If you want to buy 100 shares of the stock, you would pay $58¼ (the higher price) per share. Likewise, if you want to sell 100 shares of the stock, you would receive $58 (the lower price) per share. Some stocks that are not actively traded may not have a bid or an offer price during a particular day.

Why Buy Common Stocks?

Investors purchase common stock (equities) for two purposes: (1) dividend income (or potential dividend income) and (2) capital appreciation (profit). Of course, if the stock declines, you will suffer a capital depreciation or loss. Also, not all common stock pays a dividend. When buying stocks, find out whether the stock has been paying a dividend and whether any research firm recommends the purchase. You may want to consult with your broker or go to the public library to obtain these facts. Forecasting future stock price movement is very difficult.

Dividend Income. Dividend income is a distribution of the earnings of the corporation and is normally paid monthly or quarterly. Dividends are normally based on the corporation's profits. Many corporations offer *dividend reinvestment programs* (DRIPS) to their shareholders. Such a program allows you to purchase additional shares of stock with the cash dividend. Some corporations charge a service fee and also pass along any commissions charged by the broker executing the trade for the DRIP. Statements showing the transactions and share balances are normally mailed shortly thereafter.

Capital Appreciation. Capital appreciation occurs when the share price rises in value. The stock price changes daily based on many variable factors, including inflation rates, interest rates, unemployment, recession, economic expansion, political environment, war and psychology of the marketplace. If you are a long-term investor, you may not be too concerned with the daily fluctuations. However, if the economic outlook changes significantly, you might want to reevaluate your investment holdings. Other factors that can affect a company's stock price are revenues, earnings, dividends, new product development, management changes and overall growth of the particular industry.

How Common Stock Is Classified

Companies and their common stock are classified in numerous ways. They may be classified by investment objective, economic sector, industry, size or any other way selected by a portfolio manager. A *portfolio manager,* also known as a *money manager,* invests in stocks, bonds and other securities for corporations, individuals, pension plans, mutual funds and other organizations.

Investing in stock of different classifications provides you with a well-diversified portfolio. Because certain types of stock perform better than others during a particular market or economic cycle, it may be best that you invest in several stock types. Thus, during these cycles, part of your portfolio may outperform the general market—or, of course, may underperform the general market. However, over the long term, the volatility of the returns may even out, producing a rate of return similar to the market averages.

Figure 16.1 lists several different ways of classifying common stock. *These classifications and common stock price movements are only expectations. Future stock price performance is not guaranteed and may not act like the historical price performance.*

Analyzing Common Stock

Two basic methods are used to analyze stock: (1) fundamental analysis and (2) technical analysis.

Briefly, *fundamental analysis* uses factors such as company earnings, dividends, management and products as well as economic cycles to determine the potential valuation of a stock price. One important number is the *price-earnings (PE) ratio.* You calculate the PE ratio by

FIGURE 16.1 Common Stock Classifications

Classification	Description
Investment Objective	
Cyclical	Company earnings should coincide with the rise and fall of the economy, so the stock price should follow the economy's growth.
Defensive	Company earnings should be relatively insensitive to the ups and downs of the economy, so the stock price should hold up well during weak phases of the economic cycle.
Growth	Company earnings should grow faster than the general economy, so the stock price should exceed other stock prices, regardless of economic cycles.
Income	Company earnings are relatively stable and stock offers a high dividend yield, so the stock price should perform relative to interest rate changes. If interest rates go up, the stock price may go down, and if interest rates go down, the stock price may go up.
Special situation	The company introduces a new product line or reorganizes its structure, so the stock should perform better than previously if the special situation is successful.
Speculative	Company earnings are not stable and the financial condition is not very sound, so the company may or may not become profitable. The investment risk is typically unknown, so the stock price may or may not do well.
Industry	
Financial	Companies offer financial services, such as banks, brokerage firms, investment services, credit card companies, finance companies and insurance companies.
Industrial	Companies manufacture, sell or distribute industrial products, consumer products and services, such as autos, chemicals, clothing, computers, electrical equipment, entertainment, food, health care, paper, pharmaceuticals, photography, oil, steel, etc.
Transportation	Companies offer transportation services, such as airline companies, air freight companies, railroad companies, shipping companies and truck companies.

FIGURE 16.1   Common Stock Classifications (Continued)

Classification	Description
Utility	Companies offer public services, such as electric utility companies, gas companies and telephone companies.
Economic Sectors	
Consumer staples	Companies provide products and services for consumers, such as beverage, clothing, cosmetics, entertainment, food, health care, hotels, household items, leisure activities, pharmaceuticals, photography, restaurants, tobacco, etc.
Capital goods	Companies provide major products for industrial production or services, such as aerospace, computers, electronics, electrical equipment, machinery, etc.
Basic industries	Companies supply, distribute and manufacture materials for industrial production and consumption, including chemicals, lumber, metals, oil, paper, steel, etc.
Interest rate sensitive	Companies provide financial and public services, such as banks, electric and gas utilities, financial services, insurance companies, telephone companies, etc.
Consumer cyclicals	Companies provide major consumer goods, such as appliances, automobiles, boats, housing, etc.
Size	
Large cap	Large-cap companies typically have many shares of stock traded in the marketplace and normally are household names. These blue-chip, high-quality companies have generally been consistent with earnings, dividends and product development.
Mid cap	Mid-cap companies have fewer shares outstanding in the marketplace and normally are not as well known as large-cap companies. These second-tier companies are good quality and may have steady growth.
Small cap	Small-cap companies have fewer shares outstanding than mid-cap companies. Because many are newer companies, they may grow quickly. These third-tier companies are less well known than second-tier companies. They may offer more risk to the investor, but may also offer more return.

dividing the price per share by the earnings per share. This gives you a figure you can use to evaluate where the stock is trading relative to its earnings. A comparison of the stock's previous PE ratios may help you determine whether the stock is undervalued (possibly a good time to buy) or overvalued (possibly a good time to sell).

Technical analysis uses information such as previous trading ranges, trading volumes and trend lines to determine the valuation of a stock price.

Ranking Common Stock

When analyzing stock, you may use rankings to determine the quality of the company. Both Standard & Poor's and Moody's Investors Service rank stock based primarily on stability of earnings and record of dividend payments. The ranking is not a recommendation or a prediction of future market price; it is simply an evaluation of past stability of earnings and dividend payments.

Standard & Poor's ranks common stock according to the following designations:[1]

A+ Highest	B+ Average	C Lowest
A High	B Below average	D In reorganization
A– Above average	B– Lower	NR No ranking

Moody's ranks stock according to the following designations:[2]

High grade	Medium grade
Investment grade	Lower medium grade
Upper medium grade	Speculative grade

[1]Reprinted by permission of Standard & Poor's, a division of The McGraw-Hill Companies.

[2]Reprinted by permission of Moody's Investors Service, Inc.

See *Standard & Poor's Stock Guide* and *Moody's Handbook of Common Stocks* for further explanation of the rankings. See Appendix C, "Resources," for addresses.

Calculating Returns

In Chapter 3, you stated the rate of return you would like to achieve. A progress report usually helps determine whether you are on track in attaining your goal. Calculate your current yield, capital appreciation or loss and total return—necessary checkpoints on the way to evaluating your progress toward your overall investment objective. Annualizing your returns will allow you to compare your returns to alternative investments. See Financial Focus 1 for more on calculating returns.

Current Yield. To calculate current yield (current return), use the following formula:

$$\frac{\text{Annual dividend}}{\text{Current price}} \times 100 = \text{Current yield}$$

Expressed as a percentage, the yield represents the income return the stock provides now at the current price, based on the company's indicated annual dividend.

Capital Appreciation or Loss. To calculate profit or loss, use the following formula:

$$\text{Sale proceeds} - \text{Cost basis} = \text{Profit or loss}$$

Cost basis is the amount you paid when you originally purchased the security plus any additional purchases (including dividends reinvested). To calculate percentage profit or loss, use the following formula:

$$\frac{\text{Sales proceeds} - \text{Cost basis}}{\text{Cost basis}} \times 100 = \text{Percentage profit or loss}$$

Total Return. The total return of an investment is the sum of the dividend income and the capital appreciation or depreciation. To calculate total return, use one of the following formulas:

$$\text{Dividend income} + \text{Profit} = \text{Total return}$$

or

$$\text{Dividend income} - \text{Loss} = \text{Total return}$$

The total return percentage is the most important figure when determining your investment's overall performance. To calculate this figure, use the following formula:

$$\frac{\text{Total return}}{\text{Cost basis}} \times 100 = \text{Total return percentage}$$

Stock Certificates

When you buy stock, you have the option of receiving a stock certificate or letting the brokerage firm hold the certificate on your behalf (known as holding in *street name*). If you sell stock for which you hold a certificate, you must endorse the certificate to make it negotiable for delivery to the brokerage firm. In lieu of endorsing the certificate, you may sign a stock power, which is a form duplicating the back of the certificate. If you sell stock held in street name, you need only instruct your broker to sell the shares. The certificate is already negotiable.

When you sell stock, you have three business days to make delivery of your certificate, if you have physical possession of it. When you buy stock, you have three days to pay for the shares. If you request the certificate, it may take anywhere from three to four weeks after payment to receive it.

A *transfer agent* records the names and addresses of the owners, changes the certificate registration when the shares are transferred and pays the dividends to the appropriate owner.

Your Portfolio Investment Questions (PIQs)

Stock is available for every investment objective. Trying to narrow the selection to a few appropriate ones is time-consuming. You may read or hear about different stocks in newsletters, newspapers, books and magazines and on television. Also, your investment professional might recommend stocks to you. The following PIQs will help you uncover some of the fundamental facts about the stocks in which you are interested. You may want to complete a new PIQs form every time you purchase a different common stock.

 INVESTOR'S TIPS

- Common stock is an investment for a portion of your *investment money,* and, in some cases, for a portion of your *risk money.*
- Common stock *may* provide the *best rate of return* over the *long term.*
- Understand the *fundamental* and *technical reasons* before purchasing common stock.
- Some companies and industries perform better during a particular *market cycle* than others. Therefore, *diversify* your portfolio by *purchasing many different types of stocks,* thus giving you a better chance that some stocks will increase in value.

Selecting Common Stock

Your Portfolio Investment Questions (PIQs)

Name of investment _____ **Date** _____

1. How may I obtain a current research report or annual report?

   Name _____

   Firm _____

   Address _____ Telephone number _____

   _____ Fax number _____

2. What is the ticker symbol, and where does the common stock trade?

3. What is the company's primary business?

4. How is the company classified? (Check all appropriate answers.)

   Investment Objective

   _____ Cyclical   _____ Defensive   _____ Growth

   _____ Income   _____ Special situation   _____ Speculative

   Industry

   _____ Financial   _____ Utility–electric and gas

   _____ Industrial   _____ Utility–telephone

   _____ Transportation

   Economic Sector

   _____ Consumer staples   _____ Capital goods

   _____ Basic industries   _____ Interest rate sensitive

   _____ Consumer cyclicals

   Size

   _____ Large cap   _____ Mid cap   _____ Small cap

   Other

   _____ Other _____

Selecting Common Stock (Continued)

Your Portfolio Investment Questions (PIQs)

Name of investment _____ **Date** _____

5. What are the financial data for the company's common stock?

   A) Price per share   _____ (today's price)

   B) Earnings per share   _____ (current year)

   C) Dividends per share   _____ (current year)

6. What are the financial ratios for the company's common stock?

   A) Current dividend yield   _____

   B) Price-earnings (PE) ratio   _____

7. How does Standard & Poor's rank the common stock? (Check one.)

   _____ A+   _____ A-   _____ B   _____ C   _____ NR

   _____ A   _____ B+   _____ B-   _____ D

8. What have been the price ranges for the past year and the past three years?

9. What economic scenario could cause the common stock price to increase?

10. What economic scenario could cause the common stock price to decrease?

11. What corporate development could cause the common stock price to increase?

12. What corporate development could cause the common stock price to decrease?

13. What risks do I incur if I buy the common stock?

14. Do I want the shares of common stock to be issued in certificate form to me or held in street name in my brokerage account?

CHAPTER 17

Picking Preferred Stock

Preferred stock is an equity security issued by a corporation to raise capital to build plants, purchase equipment and expand business operations. It is considered a senior equity security because the dividends from preferred stock must be paid before the common stock shareholders receive any dividends. Also, preferred stock shareholders have prior claims to assets over common stock shareholders should the company go bankrupt. Although preferred stock represents equity ownership, preferred stock shareholders typically do not vote. Preferred stock is denoted by either "Pr" or "Pref."

Benefits of Preferred Stock

Owning preferred stock offers several benefits: (1) steady fixed income, (2) prior claim to dividends over common stock shareholders and (3) senior security to common stock shareholders. If your investment objective is to receive income, preferred stock may be suitable for you.

FIGURE 17.1   Corporation's Priority of Payment for Stocks and Bonds

Priority	Type of Security	Type of Payment
First	Bonds and notes	Interest
Second	Preferred stock	Dividends
Third	Common stock	Dividends

Dividends

Unlike common stock dividends, most preferred stock dividends are usually fixed for the life of the preferred stock. The fixed rate is based on the par value of the preferred stock. *Par value,* typically $25 per share, is the price for which the preferred stock was originally issued. The dividend may be stated as a dollar amount or as a percentage of par value and is generally paid quarterly.

If a preferred stock pays a $2 dividend, the current yield is 8 percent, based on the price of $25 at this point in time. The calculation is $(2 \div 25) \times 100 = 8\%$. See Financial Focus 1 for more on calculating returns.

Are Preferred Stocks Like Bonds?

In many ways, preferred stocks are like corporate bonds. Most preferred stocks provide fixed-dividend payments, while most bonds offer fixed-interest payments. Both may have call provisions and are rated based on the corporation's ability to pay the dividend or interest. Both securities trade similarly due to the fixed-income feature. Preferred stock prices usually decline as interest rates increase and usually rise as interest rates decrease.

However, most traditional preferred stocks do not have maturity dates like bonds and are considered perpetual. They are junior securities to bonds because the dividends for preferred stocks must be paid *after* the interest is paid to bondholders. Also, preferred stock shareholders have claims to assets only *after* the bondholders should the company go bankrupt. Figure 17.1 shows the corporation's priority of payment for bonds and stocks.

Finally, many preferred stocks trade on the NYSE, AMEX or OTC, thus providing secondary market liquidity. However, most corporate bonds do not trade on an exchange, such as the NYSE or AMEX.

Rating Preferred Stock

When you consider purchasing preferred stock, use its rating to help you evaluate the investment. Standard & Poor's and Moody's rate preferred stock primarily on the issuer's capacity and willingness to pay preferred stock dividends. Because you normally purchase preferred stock for the income return, S&P and Moody's ratings are very beneficial.

Standard & Poor's uses the following rating designations:

AAA	Highest rating—extremely strong capacity to pay dividends
AA	High quality—very strong capacity to pay dividends
A	Sound capacity to pay dividends
BBB	Adequate capacity to pay dividends
BB, B, CCC	Speculative capacity to pay dividends
CC	In arrears on paying past dividends, but currently paying
C	Currently not paying dividends
D	Currently not paying dividends and in default on debt obligations
NR	Issue is not rated

The ratings from AA to CCC may be modified by a "+" or "–."

Refer to *Standard & Poor's Stock Guide* for further explanation of the rankings. See Appendix C, "Resources," for addresses.

Source: Reprinted by permission of Standard & Poor's, a division of The McGraw-Hill Companies.

Types of Preferred Stock

In addition to having similar classifications as common stock—for example, by industry—traditional, or perpetual, preferred stock is issued with some unique features, such as cumulative, convertible and adjustable rate.

Cumulative. This type of preferred stock states that if a corporation's board of directors elects not to pay a dividend in any given quarter, the unpaid dividends must accumulate, or accrue, and must be paid to the preferred stock shareholders *before* any dividends are paid to the common stock shareholders.

Convertible. Convertible preferred stock, as the name implies, allows you to convert the security into a set number of common shares at a specified price. The conversion ratio represents the number of shares and the price per common share that the preferred stock can be converted into. It is important that you know the ratio before you decide to convert the preferred stock into common stock.

Adjustable Rate. Although most preferred stock is issued with a fixed dividend, in some cases, it is issued with an adjustable dividend rate. As interest rates change, so will the dividend rate for this type of preferred stock. The dividend rate increases as interest rates rise and decreases as interest rates decline. This provision helps stabilize the stock price during interest rate changes. However, it will either increase or decrease the income you receive.

New Types of Preferred Securities. Over the past several years, the preferred stock marketplace has changed with the addition of three new types of preferred securities: (1) Monthly Income Preferred Securities[SM] (MIPS[SM]), (2) Quarterly Income Preferred Securities[SM] (QUIPS[SM]) and (3) Trust Originated Preferred Securities[SM] (TOPrS[SM]). QUIPS, TOPrS and MIPS now constitute virtually all of the new preferred stock issues brought to market by corporations. All three preferred securities generally have set maturities, such as 30 to 50 years. You should be aware of the *dividend deferral period,* whereby an issuer of QUIPS, TOPrS or MIPS has the right to suspend dividend payments without default, typically for 18 to 60 months. It's important to know that, should the issuer elect to suspend dividend payments, it must also simultaneously suspend the dividends for the other outstanding preferred and common stock. If dividends are suspended, you may be required to pay tax on the accrued but unpaid dividends.

Your Portfolio Investment Questions (PIQs)

Although preferred stock has a name that implies specialness—i.e., "preferred"—it still has risk. However, preferred stock does have features that differentiate it from other preferred stock. Finding the answers to the following PIQs will help you learn about some of the characteristics and returns of the various types of preferred stock.

 INVESTOR'S TIPS

- Consider preferred stock for a portion of your *investment money.*
- Most preferred stock is an investment for *income* purposes.
- Remember that preferred stock is an equity security, but it (excluding convertible and adjustable-rate preferred stock) usually *trades like a bond.*
- *Preferred stock dividends* are *paid* to preferred stock shareholders *before* dividends are paid to common stock shareholders.
- Traditional preferred stock is generally callable and perpetual with no set maturity date.
- MIPS, QUIPS and TOPrS usually have long-term maturities (typically 30 to 50 years) and call features.

✎ Choosing Preferred Stock

Your Portfolio Investment Questions (PIQs)

Name of investment _____ **Date** _____

1. How may I obtain a current research report or annual report?

   Name _____

   Firm _____

   Address _____ Telephone number _____

   _____ Fax number _____

2. What is the ticker symbol, and where does the preferred stock trade?

3. What is the company's primary business?

4. How is the company's industry classified? (Check one.)

   _____ Financial   _____ Utility–electric and gas

   _____ Industrial   _____ Utility–telephone

   _____ Transportation

5. What is the preferred stock's par value?

6. What is the preferred stock's current price?

7. What is the preferred stock's dividend rate–either as a percentage or a dollar amount?

8. What is the preferred stock's current yield?

9. What are the preferred stock's call features?

✏️ Choosing Preferred Stock (Continued)

Your Portfolio Investment Questions (PIQs)

Name of investment _____ **Date** _____

10. What is the preferred stock's yield to call?

11. When are the preferred stock's dividends paid?

12. How does Standard & Poor's rate the preferred stock? (Check one.)

     _____ AAA   _____ BB   _____ C

     _____ AA   _____ B   _____ D

     _____ A   _____ CCC   _____ NR

     _____ BBB   _____ CC   _____ Other _____

13. Does the preferred stock have any special features? (Check the appropriate ones.)

     _____ Adjustable rate   _____ Cumulative

     _____ Convertible   _____ Noncumulative

     _____ Other _____

14. Is the preferred security a MIPS, QUIPS or TOPrS?

15. If the preferred stock is adjustable rate, what are the terms of the dividend rate?

16. If the preferred stock is convertible, what are the terms of conversion?

17. What is the financial data for the company's *common* stock?

     A) Price per share   _____   (today's price)

     B) Earnings per share   _____   (current year)

     C) Dividends per share   _____   (current year)

Choosing Preferred Stock (Continued)

Your Portfolio Investment Questions (PIQs)

Name of investment _____ Date _____

18. What economic scenario could cause the preferred stock price to increase?

19. What economic scenario could cause the preferred stock price to decrease?

20. What corporate development could cause the preferred stock price to increase?

21. What corporate development could cause the preferred stock price to decrease?

22. What risks do I incur if I buy the preferred stock?

23. Do I want the shares of preferred stock to be issued in certificate form to me or held in street name in my brokerage account?

Notes

CHAPTER 18

Finding Open-End Funds (Mutual Funds)

Not all mutual funds are alike. More than 350 mutual fund groups manage more than *5,500 individual funds* with distinct investment objectives and risks, to name just two important differences. You may want to take a closer look at various funds and their management styles before you invest.

An investment company's business is to invest and manage securities according to a specific investment objective(s). The investment company (fund) is organized as either a corporation or a trust. An *open-end fund,* commonly called a *mutual fund,* is one type of investment company. Typically, the fund's investment manager is a firm, whereas the fund's portfolio manager is an individual. Each fund's portfolio manager may invest in only the securities permitted by the prospectus. Depending on and limited by the investment objective(s) and fund policies, the fund may buy U.S. stocks, U.S. Treasury notes and bonds, federal agency notes and bonds, corporate notes and bonds, municipal notes and bonds, certificates of deposit, foreign stocks and bonds, and other marketable securities.

Benefits of Investing in Mutual Funds

You can enjoy many benefits by investing in mutual funds: investment income and profits earned by the fund, professional portfolio management, diversification, stated investment objective(s), access to foreign markets, dividend reinvestment, ease of buying and selling shares and exchange privileges.

Prospectus

Read the prospectus carefully before investing. Like a blueprint, the prospectus tells you everything about the fund, such as the investment objective(s), risk considerations, the investment manager, the portfolio manager, securities that the fund can purchase, investment restrictions, sales charges, management fees, expenses, procedures for buying and selling shares, shareholder services, dividend and distribution policies and past financial information. One item the prospectus does *not* tell you is the fund's future performance. A prospectus is updated once each year, so be sure you receive a current one before you invest.

Types of Funds

A fund's investment objective(s) is your key to selecting suitable funds for your portfolio. The fund's name often tells you the type of fund it is; however, the name cannot tell you everything about the fund's investment objective or the risks involved. Several types of mutual funds are stock funds, bond funds, balanced funds and asset allocation funds. You may want to allocate some of your assets among several types of mutual funds for diversification.

Stock Mutual Funds

Stock mutual funds may be broadly classified as U.S stock funds, international stock funds and global stock funds. Investors purchase stock mutual funds primarily for capital appreciation and, in some funds, secondarily for income. While these funds have generally provided good returns historically over the long term, they carry more risk to the principal over the short term. International and global stock mutual funds also carry currency risk.

U.S. Stock Funds. U.S. stock funds invest primarily in stocks of U.S. companies. Because many types of companies are traded in the marketplace, each prospectus will state the type of stocks the fund purchases and the fund's investment objective(s).

Following are some of the more common types of U.S. stock funds and why you might consider them as part of your portfolio: large-cap stock funds for capital appreciation; mid-cap stock funds for capital appreciation; small-cap stock funds for capital appreciation; large-cap and mid-cap stock funds for income and capital appreciation; dividend-paying stock funds for income; and industry stock funds for capital appreciation.

International Stock Funds. International stock funds invest primarily in stocks of international (foreign) companies. You might invest in them for capital appreciation. Following are some of the more common types of international stock funds: large-cap foreign stock funds; mid-cap foreign stock funds; small-cap foreign stock funds; emerging markets stock funds (investing in companies in developing countries); and foreign country stock funds (one, two or more particular countries). International funds usually give you more diversification than one-country international funds because international funds buy stock from several different countries. In addition to other risks, international stock funds carry currency risk.

Global Stock Funds. Global stock funds purchase stock of companies throughout the world. These funds give you more diversification than one-country funds because they buy both U.S. and international stock. In addition to other risks, global stock funds carry currency risk.

Bond Mutual Funds

In addition to investing in stock mutual funds, you might want to consider bond mutual funds. You can choose from several categories, such as U.S. bond funds, international bond funds and global bond funds. Purchased primarily for income, bond mutual funds include many varieties, such as government, municipal and corporate bond funds. The basic risks associated with bond funds are credit risk and interest rate risk. International and global bond funds also carry currency risk.

U.S. Bond Funds. These funds purchase primarily bonds issued by entities in the United States. Each fund typically buys bonds or notes of a particular range of maturities—that is, short term, intermediate term or long term. Within each of these three categories, the fund can be classified as high quality, medium quality or low quality. U.S. bond funds also can be classified as being either taxable or tax-exempt. *Taxable bond funds* invest in bonds that pay taxable interest income, such as corporate and U.S. government bonds. *Tax-exempt bond funds* invest in bonds that pay tax-exempt interest income, such as municipal bonds. Some funds invest only in municipal bonds issued by one particular state to obtain the tax benefits of that state.

High-yield or high-income bonds are commonly known as *junk bonds,* which are medium-quality to low-quality bonds that carry greater risk than investment-grade bonds. A fund's prospectus explains in more detail the ratings of bonds the fund is allowed to purchase.

International Bond Funds. These funds purchase primarily bonds issued outside of the United States, such as bonds of foreign corporations and foreign governments. They may also be classified as short term, intermediate term or long term, depending on a fund's investment objective. In addition to other risks, international bond funds carry currency risk.

Global Bond Funds. These funds purchase bonds of companies and governments throughout the world. Global funds give you more diversification than one-country funds because they buy both U.S. and international bonds. In addition to other risks, global bond funds carry currency risk.

Balanced Mutual Funds

Purchased primarily for capital appreciation and moderate income, balanced mutual funds invest in stocks and bonds. The types of stocks and bonds vary depending on a fund's investment objective. The percentage invested in each category also varies depending on the portfolio manager's market allocation and the restrictions set forth in the prospectus. The basic risks associated with balanced funds are risk of principal, credit risk and interest rate risk.

Asset Allocation Mutual Funds

Purchased primarily for total return, asset allocation mutual funds invest in stocks, bonds and money market securities. One feature of such a fund is flexibility—the fund may shift all or most of its assets into one type of security, such as all stocks or all bonds. The portfolio manager usually uses an asset allocation model to time the market. This helps him or her decide when to shift the assets. *Market timing* is the technique of trying to buy low and sell high rather than staying fully invested for the long term. The typical investment objective of an asset allocation fund is capital appreciation. The basic risks associated with the fund are risk of principal, credit risk and interest rate risk.

Net Asset Value (NAV)

The price of the fund's shares, known as the *net asset value* (NAV) per share, fluctuates based on the performance of the underlying securities held in the fund. You may buy shares from the fund and sell (redeem) shares back to the fund any business day on which the New York Stock Exchange is open.

At the close of business each day, the NAVs of all mutual funds are calculated using the following formula:

$$\frac{\text{Fund's total assets} - \text{Fund's total liabilities}}{\text{Fund's outstanding shares}} = \text{Fund's NAV per share}$$

Therefore, whether you buy or sell, you will receive that day's close-of-business price. NAVs are listed in the newspaper, usually under either "Mutual Funds" or "Investment Companies."

Costs of Buying and Selling Mutual Funds

Mutual fund companies can charge you in one of three ways for buying and selling shares: (1) front-end load, (2) contingent deferred sales charge and (3) no load. Read the prospectus for the exact sales charge schedule before investing.

Front-End Load (Class A Shares). *Front-end load* means that you pay a sales charge when you buy the shares, not when you sell them. The *offering price,* paid upon purchase, consists of the NAV and the sales charge. When you sell (*redeem*) shares, the price you receive is the NAV, also known as the *bid price.* To profit, you must sell the shares when the NAV is higher than the initial offering price you paid, excluding any dividends and capital gains paid to you.

Contingent Deferred Sales Charge (Class B Shares). *Contingent deferred sales charge* (CDSC) means that under certain circumstances you pay a sales charge when you sell the shares. Under this pricing structure, you pay no sales charge when you buy the shares and no sales charge when you sell, if you have held the shares for a certain number of years. The offering price is the NAV. However, if you sell the shares during a certain time period after you bought them, you will pay a sales charge. Generally, you can sell your shares from reinvested dividends without a sales charge. The sales charge normally is calculated on a declining scale, whereby the charge declines by a certain percentage each year. After the allotted time, you pay no sales charge when you sell.

No Load (Class C Shares). *No-load* funds have no sales charges for buying or selling the shares. The NAV and the offering price are the same.

Exchange Privilege

Usually, you can exchange shares from one fund to another without a sales charge if the funds are within the same fund family. The exchange price is normally the NAV for both funds. An important feature, this privilege allows you to move your assets to a different market if one market is not performing well.

Annual Operating Expenses

Most funds, whether they are front-end, CDSC or no-load, are charged a *management fee* by the manager for the advice and administration of the funds' assets. Also, each fund has "*other expenses,*" such as valuating the fund's securities, operating the fund, safekeeping the securities and hiring transfer agents and independent accountants.

Another annual expense may be the *12b-1 fee.* This fee covers the fund's selling costs and service fee for maintaining shareholder accounts and for personal service. If the 12b-1 fee exceeds .25 percent, the fund cannot call itself a no-load fund. Typically, CDSC funds may charge a 12b-1 fee up to 1 percent, or even more.

In the prospectus, you will find the fund's total expenses and sales charges, as well as a summary of expenses, which lists any and all sales charges, redemption fees, 12b-1 fees, exchange fees and other expenses.

Distributions

Mutual funds make *distributions* to you in the form of dividends and realized capital gains, either short term or long term. A mutual fund receives income, such as dividends and interest, from the securities held in its portfolio. After the fund has paid its expenses, it distributes to you the net income, if any. The income return, expressed as a percentage yield, is important for you to know so you may compare the fund's return to returns of alternative investments. Capital gains are distributed to you when the fund realizes a net profit from trading securities within the fund's portfolio. The Securities and Exchange Commission (SEC) has standardized the reporting of "yields" on mutual fund shares. See Financial Focus 1 for more on calculating returns.

Dividends

Mutual funds can declare dividends daily, monthly, quarterly, semi-annually or annually, depending on the fund type. You may receive the dividends in cash or have the fund automatically reinvest the cash dividends in more shares, usually without a sales charge. Dividends may be reinvested daily or when paid. Whether you receive the cash dividends or reinvest them in more shares, you must declare the dividends as income, either taxable or tax-exempt, on your tax return.

Capital Gains

When the fund sells securities and realizes a net profit, you may receive that net capital gain. If the gain is considered long term, it is paid to you at least annually and you must declare it as a long-term capital gain on your tax return. If the gain is considered short term, it is paid to you periodically and you must declare it as ordinary income on your tax return. Of course, you may receive the cash or have the fund reinvest either type of distribution in more shares, usually without a sales charge. Check with your tax adviser for further information regarding the tax consequences of mutual fund distributions.

You will realize a profit or loss when you sell your shares depending on the difference between your adjusted cost basis and the net proceeds, excluding any dividends and capital gains received.

What Are the Best Funds To Buy?

Rather than buying the "hot" funds of the year or the most publicized funds, your best course of action may be to match suitable funds to your investment objective. The funds you buy should fit into your overall portfolio and meet your risk tolerance. Additionally, mutual funds are normally purchased for the long term. Timing short-term market swings is difficult. Therefore, funds that have performed steadily may do better over the long term than some of the more volatile funds.

Your Portfolio Investment Questions (PIQs)

Many financial newspapers and magazines, as well as brokerage firms, recommend mutual funds. With more than 5,500 individual funds to select from nationwide, tracking and understanding their investment objectives, sales charges, asset allocations and other pertinent information is quite a job. The following PIQs should help you begin the process of selecting suitable funds for your portfolio. If and when you add mutual funds to your portfolio, complete a PIQs checklist for each. This will help you organize your investments by asset allocation and investment objective.

 INVESTOR'S TIPS

- Open-end funds (mutual funds) are usually an investment for a part of your *investment money* and, in some cases, for a portion of your *risk money*.
- Match *your investment objective* with the mutual *fund's investment objective*.
- Read the *full prospectus* carefully before investing and focus on the following:
  - Investment objective
  - Risk factors
  - Types of securities the fund may purchase
  - Allocation of assets
  - Current and past investment income
  - SEC yield
  - Distribution rate
  - Past performance (total return)
  - Sales charges and total operating expenses
  - Investment manager's credentials

✎ Finding Open-End Funds (Mutual Funds)

Your Portfolio Investment Questions (PIQs)

Name of investment _____ **Date** _____

1. How may I obtain a current prospectus, research report, annual report and other information?

   Name _____

   Firm _____

   Address _____ Telephone number _____

   _____ Fax number _____

2. What type of mutual fund is it? (Check one.)

   _____ U.S. stock   _____ Global balanced

   _____ U.S. bond/note–taxable   _____ International stock

   _____ U.S. bond/note–tax-exempt   _____ International bond/note

   _____ U.S. balanced   _____ International balanced

   _____ Global stock   _____ Asset allocation

   _____ Global bond/note   _____ Other _____

3. What is the fund's investment objective?

4. What securities may the fund purchase?

5. What is the quality of the underlying securities currently held in the mutual fund?

6. How long has the current portfolio manager overseen the fund?

7. What have been the "total returns" for the past one, three, five and ten years?

Finding Open-End Funds (Mutual Funds) (Continued)

Your Portfolio Investment Questions (PIQs)

Name of investment _____ **Date** _____

8. What is the fund's "SEC yield"?

9. What is the current distribution rate?

10. Is the dividend (distribution) taxable or tax-exempt?

11. What is the net asset value (NAV)?

12. What is the offering price?

13. Under what pricing structure does the fund operate? (Check one.)

    _____ Front-end load

    _____ Contingent deferred sales charge

    _____ No load

14. What sales charges or fees will I incur if I sell fund shares?

15. What are the total operating expenses?

16. How do I go about having dividends and capital gains reinvested? What will I pay to do so?

17. How do I go about exchanging fund shares? What will I pay to do so?

✐ Finding Open-End Funds (Mutual Funds) (Continued)

Your Portfolio Investment Questions (PIQs)

Name of investment _____ Date _____

18. What economic scenario could cause the fund's net asset value to increase?

19. What is my potential gain if I purchase the fund?

20. What economic scenario could cause the fund's net asset value to decrease?

21. What is my potential loss if I purchase the fund?

22. Do I want the shares of the mutual fund to be issued in certificate form to me, held at the mutual fund's transfer agent or held in street name in my brokerage account?

Notes

CHAPTER 19

Choosing Closed-End Funds

More than 500 closed-end funds are available for purchase. Because some closed-end funds are bargains and some are not, check out the NAV, the market price, valuation, performance and investment objectives.

Organized either as a corporation or a trust, an *investment company* (fund) invests in and manages securities according to a specific investment objective. Typically, the fund's investment manager is a firm, whereas the fund's portfolio manager is an individual. Each fund's portfolio manager may invest in only the securities permitted by the prospectus, such as U.S. stocks, U.S. Treasury notes and bonds, federal agency notes and bonds, corporate notes and bonds, municipal notes and bonds, certificates of deposit, foreign stocks and bonds and other marketable securities.

A *closed-end fund* is one type of investment company. A prospectus is issued when the closed-end fund offers stock (shares of beneficial interest) to the public through an initial public offering (IPO). The investment manager then invests the money raised from the IPO according to the prospectus. After the initial offering, the fund is "closed" and no more shares are offered to the public. Shares are then traded in the secondary market, such as the New York Stock Exchange (NYSE), the American Stock Exchange (AMEX) or the Nasdaq Stock Market[SM]. At this point, if you want to buy shares, you must buy them from other shareholders in the marketplace. Likewise, shareholders who want to liquidate shares must sell them there.

Benefits of Investing in Closed-End Funds

The benefits of investing in closed-end funds are professional portfolio management, diversification, stated investment objective(s), reinvestment of dividends, access to foreign markets and ease of buying and selling shares. Like the price of underlying securities in the portfolio, the closed-end fund's price may fluctuate, causing your investment to be either profitable or unprofitable. Also, the dividends paid to you, if any, may fluctuate.

Prospectus

Read the prospectus carefully before investing. Like the prospectus for an open-end fund, a closed-end fund prospectus notes the investment objective(s), risk considerations, investment manager, portfolio manager, securities the portfolio manager can purchase, investment restrictions, selling charges, management fees, expenses, procedures for buying and selling shares, shareholder services and dividend and distribution policies. However, the prospectus does *not* tell you the fund's future performance. If you consider buying shares of a closed-end fund via an initial public offering (IPO), ask your broker for a prospectus and read it carefully before investing. If you consider buying shares in the marketplace (after the IPO), read a research report before investing. You can obtain a research report about the fund from your broker or a research service firm. You can also obtain annual and semiannual financial reports from the fund manager.

Types of Funds

A fund's investment objective is key to selecting suitable funds for your portfolio. The fund's name sometimes, but not always, tells you what type of fund it is; however, the name cannot tell you everything about the fund's investment objective or the risks involved. You can choose from several types of closed-end funds, such as stock funds, bond funds and balanced funds.

Closed-End Stock Funds

Closed-end stock funds may be broadly classified as U.S stock funds, international stock funds and global stock funds. Investors purchase closed-end stock funds primarily for capital appreciation and secondarily for income. While these funds have generally provided good returns historically over the long term, they carry more risk of principal over the short term than over the long term. International and global stock funds also carry currency risk.

U.S. Stock Funds. U.S. stock funds invest primarily in stocks of U.S. companies. Each fund states what type of stocks it can purchase and the fund's investment objectives. Following are some of the more common types of stock funds and the reasons for investment: large-cap stock funds for capital appreciation; mid-cap stock funds for capital appreciation; small-cap stock funds for capital appreciation; large-cap and mid-cap stock funds for income and capital appreciation; and dividend-paying stock funds for income.

International Stock Funds. International stock funds invest primarily in stocks of international (foreign) companies. You might invest in them for capital appreciation. Following are some of the more common types of international stock funds: large-cap foreign stock funds; mid-cap foreign stock funds; small-cap foreign stock funds; emerging markets stock funds (investing in companies in developing countries) and foreign country stock funds (one, two or more particular countries). In addition to other risks, international stock funds carry currency risk.

Global Stock Funds. Global stock funds purchase stocks of companies throughout the world. Global stock funds give you more diversification than one-country funds because they buy both U.S. and international stocks. In addition to other risks, global stock funds carry currency risk.

Closed-End Bond Funds

In addition to investing in closed-end stock funds, you might want to consider closed-end bond funds. You can choose from several categories, including U.S. bond funds, international bond funds and global bond funds. Purchased primarily for income, closed-end bond funds include many varieties, such as government, municipal and corporate bond funds. The basic risks associated with all bond funds are credit risk and interest rate risk. International and global bond funds also carry currency risk.

U.S. Bond Funds. These funds purchase primarily bonds issued by entities in the United States. Bond funds include a wide variety of funds, such as U.S. government, municipal and corporate bond funds. Each fund typically buys bonds or notes of a particular range of maturities—that is, generally intermediate term or long term. Within each category, the fund can be classified as high quality, medium quality or low quality. U.S. bond funds also can be classified as being either taxable or tax-exempt. *Taxable bond funds* invest in bonds that pay taxable interest income, such as corporate and U.S. government bonds. *Tax-exempt bond funds* invest in bonds that pay tax-exempt interest income, such as municipal bonds. Some funds invest only in municipal bonds issued by one particular state to obtain the tax benefits of that state.

High-yield or high-income bonds are commonly known as *junk bonds,* which are medium-quality to low-quality bonds that carry a greater credit risk than investment-grade bonds. A fund's prospectus explains in more detail the ratings of the bonds the fund is allowed to purchase.

International Bond Funds. These funds purchase primarily bonds issued by entities outside of the United States, such as bonds of foreign corporations and foreign governments. They may also be classified as short term, intermediate term or long term, depending on a fund's investment objective. In addition to other risks, international bond funds carry currency risk.

Global Bond Funds. These funds purchase bonds of companies and governments throughout the world. Global funds give you more diversification than one-country funds because they buy both U.S. and international bonds. In addition to other risks, global bond funds carry currency risk.

Closed-End Balanced Funds

Purchased primarily for capital appreciation and moderate income, balanced funds invest in stocks and bonds. The types of stocks and bonds vary depending on a fund's investment objective. The percentage invested in each category also varies depending on the portfolio manager's market allocation and the restrictions set forth in the prospectus. The basic risks associated with this type of fund are risk of principal, credit risk and interest rate risk. International and global balanced funds also carry currency risk.

Market Price vs. NAV

The net asset value—not the market price—changes according to the performance of the securities the fund holds. At the close of business each week, the NAVs of closed-end funds are calculated using the following formula:

$$\frac{\text{Fund's total assets} - \text{Fund's total liabilities}}{\text{Fund's outstanding shares}} = \text{Fund's NAV per share}$$

You can find the NAVs weekly in the major financial newspapers.

Shares of closed-end funds trade like shares of common stock in the marketplace. Buyers and sellers determine a fund's market price based on the supply and demand of the shares in the marketplace. Price quotations are listed in the newspaper under the appropriate marketplace, such as the NYSE, AMEX or OTC. The normal price variation of a share is normally ⅛ of a dollar, or $.125, per share. One point equals $1 when quoting share prices. For example, if a share is priced at 15⅜, the cost of 100 shares is $1,537.50 (100 × 15.375) plus commission.

Share prices are quoted with a *bid price* and an *offer (asked) price.* The bid price is the highest price a buyer will pay for the shares; the offer price is the lowest price a seller will take for the shares. Therefore, when you sell shares, you receive the bid price; when you buy shares, you pay the offer price. A share could be quoted like this: 13 (bid) – 13¼ (offer). If you want to buy 100 shares of the fund at the market, you would pay $13¼ (the higher price) per share. Likewise, if you want to sell 100 shares of the fund at the market, you would receive $13 (the lower price) per share.

The fund is considered to be *selling at a discount* if the market price is *less than* the NAV. The fund is considered *selling at a premium* if the market price is *more than* the NAV. When investors are optimistic, increased buying may occur, which may drive prices to premiums. When investors are pessimistic, increased selling may occur, which may drive prices to discounts. Consequently, you will buy more assets for less money when you purchase closed-end bond funds at a discount. The advantage of buying closed-end funds at a discount is twofold: (1) If the market value of the underlying securities rises, the NAV of the underlying portfolio increases and if valuation (discount or premium) remains unchanged, then the share price in the marketplace increases by a similar amount. (2) You may enjoy a significant benefit when the NAV increases and the discount to the NAV narrows; the share price would outperform the fund's NAV and portfolio.

However, even if this share price seems a bargain, it is important to consider market trends because the fund's underlying securities may also decline, which would lower the NAV. This could produce more selling, thus driving the market price down even more. If the quality of any fund you hold changes, review your investment goals to make sure the fund is still appropriate for you.

Costs of Buying and Selling Closed-End Funds

You will incur commissions when you buy and sell shares of closed-end funds in the marketplace, just like you do when you buy and sell shares of stock. If you buy shares in an initial public offering, the purchase price includes an underwriting fee, which is paid to the selling broker; however, you do not pay an additional commission on the shares. The underwriting fee reduces the amount of money placed in the fund to be managed. Thus, the initial NAV of the fund will be less than the initial offering price. All closed-end funds charge a management fee and other expenses for managing and operating the funds.

Distributions

Closed-end funds make *distributions* to you in the form of dividends and realized capital gains, either short term or long term. A closed-end fund receives income, such as dividends and interest, from the securities held in its portfolio. After the fund has paid its expenses, it distributes to you the net income, if any. The income return, expressed as a percentage yield, is important for you to know so you may compare the fund's return to returns of alternative investments. Capital gains will be distributed to you at least annually when the fund realizes a net profit from trading securities within the fund's portfolio. See Financial Focus 1 for more on calculating returns.

Dividends

Closed-end funds can declare dividends monthly, quarterly, semi-annually or annually, depending on the type of fund. Bond funds usually pay dividends monthly. You may receive the dividends in cash or have the fund automatically reinvest the cash dividends in more shares, usually without a sales charge. Fund shares may have to be registered in your name in order for you to reinvest dividends. Whether you receive the cash dividends or reinvest them in more shares, you must declare the dividends as income, either taxable or tax-exempt, on your tax return. The current yield is determined by dividing the annualized income by the current bid price.

Capital Gains

The fund pays you any capital gain it realizes at least annually. If the gain is considered long term, you must declare it as a long-term capital gain on your tax return. If the gain is considered short term, it is paid to you periodically and you must declare it as ordinary income on your tax return. Of course, you may receive the cash or have the fund reinvest either type of distribution in more shares, usually without a sales charge. Check with your tax adviser for further information regarding the tax consequences of closed-end fund distributions.

You will realize a profit or loss when you sell your shares, depending on the difference between your adjusted cost basis and the net proceeds, excluding any dividends and capital gains paid (which are both taxed in the year realized).

Leveraged vs. Unleveraged Funds

One way for a portfolio manager to increase income return is to leverage the closed-end fund. The fund raises additional capital usually by issuing short-term, adjustable-rate preferred stock. This capital is then invested in longer-term securities. Because long-term interest rates are generally higher than short-term interest rates, the interest earned on investments usually exceeds the borrowing expense paid on the preferred stock or other short-term borrowings. You receive this "extra income," giving you more money than you would have earned if the fund had not been leveraged. However, depending on interest rate changes, the fund may experience a decline in its extra income, which will lower the income you receive. Additionally, the leveraged fund will likely be more volatile than a comparable unleveraged fund. Generally, leverage is a double-edged sword. When markets rise, leverage will increase profits; when markets decline, leverage will increase losses.

Your Portfolio Investment Questions (PIQs)

Closed-end funds publish a prospectus for the initial public offering (IPO). After the IPO, most closed-end fund shares are listed on the exchanges, and the funds generally publish annual and semiannual reports, not additional prospectuses. In addition, research reports may be available once the shares are listed. The following PIQs will help you understand the pricing, yields and investment objective of a particular fund. As with your other investments, anytime you consider buying a closed-end fund, complete the PIQs checklist for a good summary of the fund.

 INVESTOR'S TIPS

- Closed-end funds are usually an investment for a portion of your *investment money* and, in some cases, for a portion of your *risk money*.
- *Read* carefully the full original prospectus (if available), the fund's annual and semiannual reports, or research report and focus on the following:
  - Investment objective
  - Risk factors
  - Types of securities the fund may purchase
  - Allocation of assets
  - Current and past investment income
  - Current yield (distribution rate)
  - Past performance (total return)
  - Sales charges and total operating expenses
  - Investment manager's credentials
- Buying closed-end funds at a *discount* may give you *better value*.

When market price is greater than NAV, the price is at a premium.

NET ASSET VALUE (NAV) PER SHARE

When market price is less than NAV, the price is at a discount.

✏️ Choosing Closed-End Funds

Your Portfolio Investment Questions (PIQs)

Name of investment _____ **Date** _____

1. How may I obtain a current prospectus, research report or annual report?

   Name _____

   Firm _____

   Address _____ Telephone number _____

   _____ Fax number _____

2. What type of closed-end fund is it? (Check one.)

   ____ U.S. stock   ____ Global balanced

   ____ U.S. bond/note–taxable   ____ International stock

   ____ U.S. bond/note–tax-exempt   ____ International bond/note

   ____ U.S. balanced   ____ International balanced

   ____ Global stock   ____ Asset allocation

   ____ Global bond/note   ____ Other _____

3. What is the fund's investment objective?

4. What securities may the fund purchase?

5. What is the quality of the underlying securities the fund currently holds?

6. How long has the current portfolio manager overseen the fund?

7. Describe the fund's performance for the past one, three, five and ten years.

8. What is the fund's net asset value?

Choosing Closed-End Funds (Continued)

Your Portfolio Investment Questions (PIQs)

Name of investment _____ Date _____

9. What is the fund's market price?

10. Is the fund selling at a discount or a premium? Why?

11. What is the fund's current dividend in dollars?

12. What is the fund's current dividend as a percentage yield?

13. Is the dividend taxable or tax-exempt?

14. What commission do I incur if I buy or sell fund shares?

15. Is the fund leveraged or unleveraged?

16. If the fund is leveraged, what is the added risk?

17. What economic scenario could cause the net asset value to increase?

18. What is my potential gain if I purchase the fund?

19. What economic scenario could cause the net asset value to decrease?

20. What is my potential loss if I purchase the fund?

21. Do I want the shares of the closed-end fund to be issued in certificate form to me or held in street name in my brokerage account?

CHAPTER 20

Understanding Unit Investment Trusts

If Wall Street wants to package a particular group of securities, the unit investment trust is one of the answers! Almost all types of securities may be placed in a unit investment trust (UIT) portfolio, in accordance with the type of trust and its objectives.

An investment company, organized as a corporation or a trust, invests in and manages securities according to a specific investment objective. A *unit investment trust* is a type of investment company in which you purchase units rather than shares. Typically each unit is sponsored by one or more investment firms, which select and invest in only the securities permitted by the prospectus. Depending on the investment objective, the UIT may buy U.S. stocks, U.S. Treasury notes and bonds, federal agency notes and bonds, corporate notes and bonds, municipal notes and bonds, certificates of deposit, foreign stocks and bonds, and other marketable securities.

The sponsor selects the trust's portfolio but does not actively manage it like a mutual fund or a closed-end fund. Therefore, the portfolio is basically fixed until the trust terminates, the date of which varies for different types of trusts. The sponsor terminates the trust based on a predetermined date or, in the case of a bond trust, no later than the date of the last maturing note or bond. The sponsor may sell a particular security in the trust if the security fails to meet the criteria the trust has established.

Benefits of Investing in UITs

You can enjoy many benefits when you invest in unit investment trusts: professional selection of a securities portfolio, diversification, stated investment objective, reinvestment of distributions, access to foreign markets and ease of buying and selling units.

Like the underlying securities in the portfolio, the UIT's net asset value may fluctuate, causing your investment to increase or decrease in value. Also, the distributions paid to you, if any, may fluctuate.

Prospectus

Read the prospectus carefully before investing. Among other things, it describes the trust's investment objective, risk factors, sponsor, securities the sponsor is allowed to select, sales charges, total expenses, procedures for buying and selling units, trust's termination date and dividend and distribution policies. Of course, the prospectus cannot predict the trust's future performance.

The trust's investment objective is key to your selection of a trust. The trust's name usually denotes the type of trust it is, but it cannot tell you everything about the investment objective or the risks involved.

Types of Trusts

You can choose from two basic types of UITs, stock UITs and bond UITs.

Stock UITs

UITs may be broadly classified as consisting of U.S. stocks, international stocks and global stocks. Investors purchase stock UITs primarily to seek capital appreciation and secondarily for income. While these UITs may have generally provided good returns historically over the long term, they carry more risk of principal over the short term. International and global stock UITs also carry currency risk.

U.S. Stock UITs. Equity UITs invest in stocks of U.S. companies. Each trust prospectus states what type of stocks it can purchase and the trust's investment objective. Following are some of the more common types of stock trust funds and the reasons you might invest in them: large-cap stock trusts for appreciation; industry stock trusts (one or two specific industries) for capital appreciation; specialized stock trusts (based on a certain portfolio management theory) for capital appreciation and preferred stock trusts for income.

International Stock UITs. International equity UITs invest in stocks of international (foreign) companies. Following are some of the more common types of international stock trusts and the reasons for investment: large-cap foreign stock trusts for capital appreciation; foreign industry stock trusts (one or two specific industries) for capital appreciation; and specialized foreign stock trusts (based on a certain portfolio management theory) for capital appreciation. International stock UITs carry currency risk.

Bond UITs

In addition to investing in stock UITs, you might want to consider the many types of bond UITs. You can choose from several categories of trusts, consisting of U.S. bonds, international bonds and global bonds. Purchased primarily for income, bond UITs include many varieties, such as government, municipal and corporate bonds. The basic risks associated with all bond UITs are credit risk and interest rate risk. International and global bond UITs also carry currency risk.

U.S. Bond UITs. These UITs purchase primarily debt securities issued by entities in the United States. Each trust typically purchases bonds or notes that fall into a particular category of maturities–that is, short term, intermediate term or long term. Within each category, the trust can be classified as high quality, medium quality or low quality. U.S. bond trusts also can be classified as being either taxable or tax-exempt. *Taxable bond UITs* invest in bonds that pay taxable interest income, such as corporate and U.S. government bonds. *Tax-exempt bond UITs* invest in bonds that pay tax-exempt interest income, such as municipal bonds. Some UITs invest only in municipal bonds issued by one particular state to obtain state income tax benefits. Each bond UIT's prospectus explains in detail the ratings of the bonds in the portfolio.

International Bond UITs. International bond UITs purchase primarily bonds issued by entities outside of the United States, such as bonds of foreign corporations and foreign governments. They may also be classified as short term, intermediate term or long term, depending on a fund's investment objective. International bond UITs carry currency risk.

Costs of Buying and Selling UITs

The net asset value (NAV) fluctuates according to the performance of the underlying securities held in the portfolio. The NAV is calculated as follows:

$$\frac{\text{Trust's total assets} - \text{Trust's total liabilities}}{\text{Trust's number of outstanding units}} = \text{Trust's NAV per unit}$$

You may buy units from the trust and sell (redeem) units back to the trust on any business day. Generally, you pay a sales charge to buy units in the UIT, but no sales charge to sell (redeem) the units, unless a deferred sales charge is applicable. The sales charge is added to the NAV to determine the public offering price. The NAVs of most unit trusts are calculated each day at the close of business. Therefore, whether you buy or sell, you will receive that day's close-of-business price. Your profit or loss when you sell (redeem) the units depends on the difference between your adjusted cost basis and the net proceeds received, excluding income received. Although you cannot obtain price quotations from newspapers, you can get them from your broker or account statement.

You pay no management fee because the portfolio is fixed and unmanaged. Fees for securities valuation, supervision and administration are generally charged to the trust. The prospectus details the unit investment trust's total expenses.

Distributions

Unit investment trust funds make *distributions* to you from income received, such as dividends and interest from the securities held in its portfolio and the proceeds of sale of securities, including any capital gains, not used for redemption of units, less fees and expenses. The income return, expressed as a percentage return, is important for you to know so you may compare it to alternative investments. Typically, the prospectus states the estimated current and long-term return as of the date of the prospectus. Principal and any capital gains are normally distributed to you when the UIT sells a security from the portfolio. See Financial Focus 1 for more on calculating returns.

Dividends

Unit investment trusts can pay dividends monthly, quarterly, semi-annually or annually, depending on the type of trust and the distribution options offered. You may receive the dividends in cash or have the trust automatically reinvest the cash dividends in additional units or in another UIT. Dividend reinvestment usually requires no sales charge.

Capital Gains

The trust pays you any capital gain it realizes. Of course, you may receive the cash or have the trust automatically reinvest the distribution in additional units, usually without a sales charge.

Principal Payments

When a security held in the unit trust is sold or redeemed, the trust generally pays the proceeds to you based on the number of units you hold on a pro-rata basis. Bond UITs, especially, have bonds called or redeemed, thus providing you with payments that are considered a return of principal. Be aware of what portions are principal rather than income when you receive your distribution checks.

You will receive the NAV of the securities held in the UIT's portfolio on the trust's termination date. Therefore, it is important for you to know the termination date and the portfolio's NAV during the life of the trust.

Your Portfolio Investment Questions (PIQs)

Understanding the investment objective of a unit investment trust is extremely important, especially because a UIT's portfolio is not actively managed. Usually you may redeem the units at current market value prior to termination, or you may hold them until the termination date. The following PIQs can help you decide whether to buy a particular UIT.

INVESTOR'S TIPS

- Unit investment trusts are usually an investment for a portion of your *investment money* and, in some cases, for a portion of your *risk money.*
- Unit investment trusts are *unmanaged portfolios.*
- Purchase unit investment trusts that *match* your *investment objectives.*
- Pay attention to the UIT's termination date.
- Read the *full prospectus* carefully before investing and focus on the following:
  - Investment objective(s)
  - Risk factors
  - Types of securities that may be deposited in the portfolio
  - Actual portfolio composition
  - Estimated current return
  - Estimated long-term return
  - Sales charges, fees and expenses
  - Identity of sponsor, trustee and auditor
  - Tax considerations

Understanding UITs

Your Portfolio Investment Questions (PIQs)

Name of investment _____ **Date** _____

1. How may I obtain a current prospectus, annual report or other information?

   Name _____

   Firm _____

   Address _____ Telephone number _____

   _____ Fax number _____

2. What is the trust's investment objective?

3. What type of unit investment trust is it? (Check one.)

   _____ U.S. stock   _____ International stock

   _____ U.S. bond/note–taxable   _____ International bond/note

   _____ U.S. bond/note–tax-exempt   _____ Other _____

   _____ U.S. balanced

4. What securities may the trust purchase?

5. What firm (sponsor) will select and purchase the securities for the trust?

6. What is the quality of the underlying securities currently held in the trust?

7. What is the trust's current net asset value?

8. What is the trust's offering price?

✎ Understanding UITs (Continued)

Your Portfolio Investment Questions (PIQs)

Name of investment _____ **Date** _____

9. What sales charges or fees will I incur if I buy the units, and is any portion deferred?

10. What is the trust's estimated current return?

11. What is the trust's estimated long-term return?

12. When will the trust terminate at the latest?

13. What sales charges or fees will I incur if I sell the units prior to termination of the trust?

14. What economic scenario could cause the trust's net asset value to increase?

15. What is my potential gain if I purchase the trust?

16. What economic scenario could cause the trust's net asset value to decrease?

17. What is my potential loss if I purchase the trust?

18. Do I want the units of the trust to be issued in certificate form to me, held at the trust's transfer agent or held in street name in my brokerage account?

CHAPTER 21

Putting Limited Partnerships in Perspective

Many limited partnerships are available, but you need to know how to select a suitable one. The questions in this chapter can help you know what to look for in a limited partnership.

A partnership is one type of business organization. A *limited partnership* has one general partner (GP) and many limited partners (LPs). The *general partner* sells units to investors, who then become *limited partners*. The general partner holds all responsibility for the operations of the partnership, such as investing the capital raised, managing the partnership's business and performing the necessary accounting procedures. The general partner must act as a "fiduciary" for the limited partners and perform all actions that are in the best interest of all partners. Typically, limited partnerships invest in airplanes, equipment leasing, oil and gas, or real estate. Each has its own economic considerations, so analyze the business operations of any partnership you consider.

Prospectus

Read the prospectus carefully before investing. In it, you will find the financial terms, sales charges, expenses, conflicts of interest, business description of the partnership, investment objectives, risk considerations and tax considerations. Typically, the general partner and the limited partners share in the partnership's profits, losses, income and tax benefits based on the terms of the partnership agreement. Limited partners usually do not risk more than their original invested capital.

General Partner

The general partner receives a management fee and may earn commissions from partnership transactions. Also, the GP may be reimbursed for expenses incurred in operating the partnership. It is important to know who the general partner is, as well as the general partner's financial condition and ability to operate the partnership. You are investing in the general partner's program, so the GP's management abilities may mean the difference between profit and loss. The general partner has no control over economic conditions, market conditions or tax law changes, which can affect partnership results.

Types of Limited Partnerships

Basically, you can purchase two types of limited partnerships: direct participation programs and master limited partnerships.

Direct Participation Programs (DPPs). These programs are "private" limited partnerships where the units do not normally have a liquid secondary market. This investment is designed to be held long term until the partnership terminates. In many cases, this may be 10 to 15 years and sometimes longer.

Master Limited Partnerships (MLPs). These partnerships are "public" limited partnerships where the units have a secondary market and normally will trade on the NYSE, AMEX or Nasdaq Stock Market^{SM}. MLPs provide some of the same investment characteristics—gains, losses and income—as DPPs. Master limited partnerships are usually formed in two ways: (1) combining several DPPs that have the same business operation and the same general partner and (2) distributing a portion of a corporation's assets to form an MLP.

Tax Considerations

The distributions by both DPPs and MLPs fall under different tax-reporting requirements than do the distributions from corporations. Therefore, check with your tax adviser to determine whether limited partnerships are appropriate for your tax situation.

Your Portfolio Investment Questions (PIQs)

A limited partnership usually has a very long, detailed prospectus. Of course, you should read the prospectus carefully before you invest. However, a few basic PIQs can help you decide whether a particular partnership may suit you and warrants further analysis of the prospectus.

INVESTOR'S TIPS

- Limited partnerships are usually an investment for a portion of your *risk money* and, in some cases, for a portion of your *investment money*.
- Master limited partnerships (MLPs) are *marketable* and liquid, whereas direct participation partnerships (DPPs) are *not readily marketable*.
- Read the full prospectus and focus on the following:
  - Investment objective(s)
  - Risk factors
  - Type of business
  - Current return
  - Tax benefits
  - Sales charges and expenses
  - Sharing arrangement between limited partners and general partner
  - General partner's credentials
  - Partnership's holding period

✏️ Putting LPs in Perspective

Your Portfolio Investment Questions (PIQs)

Name of investment _____ **Date** _____

1. How may I obtain a current prospectus, research report or annual report?

   Name _____

   Firm _____

   Address _____ Telephone number _____

   _____ Fax number _____

2. Is the limited partnership a direct participation program or a master limited partnership?

3. What is the partnership's classification? (Check one.)

   _____ Real estate   _____ Leasing

   _____ Oil and gas   _____ Other _____

4. What kinds of properties will the partnership purchase?

5. Are the properties already purchased, or will they be acquired after the initial offering of units?

6. What sales charges or fees will I incur if I buy the units?

7. What is the expected life of the partnership?

8. Is there a market where I can sell the units? If so, what market?

9. What sales charges or fees will I incur if I sell the units?

✏️ Putting LPs in Perspective (Continued)

Your Portfolio Investment Questions (PIQs)

Name of investment _____ Date _____

10. Who is the general partner of the partnership?

11. What is the general partner's financial condition?

12. How long has the general partner been in business?

13. What is the sharing arrangement between the general partner and the limited partners?

14. What is the expected cash distribution, and how often can I expect to receive it?

15. What are the tax benefits?

16. Will the general partner borrow money to purchase the properties (leveraged), or will the general partner use ready cash to purchase the properties?

17. What are the other costs for organizing and managing the partnership?

18. What economic scenario could cause the value of the partnership to increase?

19. What is my potential gain if I purchase the partnership?

Putting LPs in Perspective (Continued)

Your Portfolio Investment Questions (PIQs)

Name of investment _____ **Date** _____

20. What economic scenario could cause the value of the partnership to decrease?

21. What is my potential loss if I purchase the partnership?

22. What risks are associated with owning this limited partnership?

Notes

CHAPTER 22

Grasping Managed Futures

The growth of managed futures has been so rapid over the past several years that they are becoming an asset class like stocks, bonds and money market securities. Consequently, you may want to study this area.

The term *managed futures* is derived from investors using professional money managers to trade in futures and forward contracts. *Futures and forward contracts* may represent agricultural products, bonds, cattle, currencies, financial instruments, gold, hogs, oil, silver, stock indexes and so on. We say "contracts" instead of "securities" because they are actually contracts of delivery or receipt for a particular commodity between the seller and buyer of the contracts. You may trade these contracts individually, assuming all of the potential risk and reward for each contract, or invest collectively with other individuals in a managed account or fund, thus sharing the potential risk and rewards of many different contracts among investors. Trading *individually* in futures and forward markets can be very risky and speculative, but it can also be very profitable. Managed futures are an investment for a portion of your *risk money*. Both ways are risky and speculative and should involve risk capital only. However, if your objective is to diversify among many markets, managed futures may suit your needs.

Benefits of Investing in Managed Futures

Managed futures investments offer you diversification among many global futures and forward markets. They also provide professional management with a defined trading system or a system that allows manager discretion. Because the futures and foreign currency markets are generally considered the most volatile markets, investing in these markets through a managed futures vehicle may reduce the volatility and risks normally associated with trading the contracts individually.

Hedgers and Speculators

Two categories of investors trade futures and forward markets: hedgers and speculators. Although they trade for different reasons, both are vital for the markets to survive and trade efficiently.

Briefly, as the name implies, *hedgers* want to minimize their risk of price changes for the products they produce or harvest, such as gas, oil, cattle, coffee, corn, cotton, hogs, orange juice, sugar and wheat. Some hedgers are portfolio managers who want to minimize risk by hedging their bond or stock portfolios. World currencies are used as a hedge against dollar fluctuations. *Speculators,* on the other hand, trade futures and forward markets in an attempt to profit from price movements.

Managed Futures Funds

Another way you can participate in the futures and forward markets is to invest in a managed futures fund. You may purchase units in the fund, which is usually organized as a limited partnership, through brokerage firms. The usual investment objective of a managed futures fund is to provide long-term capital appreciation and noncorrelated performance potential. You do not typically receive any income from the fund. Managed futures investments are considered *noncorrelated assets,* meaning that their price movements do not coincide with price movements of other assets. For example, if the stock market goes down, different futures markets may go down; some may not. This characteristic can benefit you because your managed futures funds may perform well when your other investments are not performing well. Managed futures' returns may be volatile over the short term. You need a long-term approach for more accurate evaluation.

General Partner and Commodity Trading Advisers

Managed futures funds typically employ a general partner (GP) to handle all administrative functions. The GP usually hires several Commodity Trading Advisers (CTAs) to trade the fund's assets. The GP will select a CTA firm—which specializes in trading futures and forward contracts—based on its methodology, past performance, standard deviation (risks associated with that performance), financial condition and management personnel. CTAs usually follow a proprietary trading methodology or discipline. The GP monitors the CTA firm's trading activities to ensure it trades according to its stated trading methods. The key to a profitable managed futures fund is the CTA's ability to make profitable trades consistently and to preserve capital during adverse market conditions.

Trading Analysis

Trend Following. Many CTAs use a *trend-following* method whereby they buy or sell a contract once they can discern that a perceived trend has been established in the price of the futures or forward contract.

Fundamental Analysis. Other CTAs use *fundamental analysis* to determine when to buy or sell a particular futures or forward contract. Fundamental analysis examines such factors as inflation, fiscal policies, monetary policies, interest rates, political conditions, currency flows, supply and demand of commodities, weather conditions and so on.

Technical Analysis. CTAs using *technical analysis* evaluate historical market data, trading volume and price ranges for the prices of the commodity contracts. Both trend followers and fundamental analysts usually use technical analysis when developing trading parameters.

Prospectus

Read the prospectus carefully before investing. It clearly defines all the sales charges, expenses, commissions, incentive fees, conflicts of interest, investment objectives, risk considerations, tax considerations, CTA's past performance figures, marketability of the units and trading methodology associated with a public futures fund.

Buying and Selling Managed Futures Funds

When you buy and sell managed futures funds be aware of those sales charges, fees and expenses that will affect your profit (or loss). Also know that the fund's NAV will be key in your buy and sell decisions.

Net Asset Value (NAV)

The units in a managed futures fund are priced according to the net asset value. The NAV is the fund's price and will fluctuate based on the performance of the fund's underlying contracts. Note that the NAV may swing widely due to the volatility of the underlying futures or forward contracts.

Sales Charges

Managed futures funds are sold either with or without a front-end load. If you pay a front-end load, a sales charge is added to the NAV to determine the offering price. If you do not have to pay a front-end load, you buy the units at NAV. However, the fund may have a redemption charge that declines to 0 percent after a certain number of years. Some general partners permit an exchange from one futures fund to another within the group without a sales charge.

Other Fees and Expenses

The futures fund may pay management fees and incentive fees to the CTAs and commissions to commodity brokers executing orders for the CTAs. The trading adviser must make a significant profit before you can earn a reasonable return. Most prospectuses document the "break-even" point for each investment to help you evaluate those fees.

Your Portfolio Investment Questions (PIQs)

Many retail investors are unfamiliar with managed futures funds—a rapidly growing part of the institutional market and also among IRA (individual retirement account) investors. The following PIQs can help you decide whether a particular fund suits you.

 INVESTOR'S TIPS

- Managed futures funds are an investment for a portion of your *risk money.*
- Managed futures funds provide you with *access* to many *global markets.*
- If you allocate a portion of your assets to this noncorrelated investment category, your total portfolio may achieve a better return with reduced risk. ("Noncorrelated" means managed futures markets will *not* perform the same as stock and bond markets.)
- Read the full prospectus carefully and focus on the following:
  - Investment objective(s)
  - Risk factors
  - Types of futures and forward markets the fund can trade
  - Past performance, if any, of the CTA(s)
  - Sales charges and expenses, including incentive fees to CTAs
  - CTA's qualifications

✏️ Grasping Managed Futures

Your Portfolio Investment Questions (PIQs)

Name of investment _____ Date _____

1. How may I obtain a current prospectus, research report or annual report?

   Name _____

   Firm _____

   Address _____ Telephone number _____

   _____ Fax number   _____

2. What is the fund's investment objective?

3. What futures and forward markets may the fund trade?

4. Who is the fund's general partner?

5. Who is/are the fund's Commodity Trading Adviser(s), CTA(s)?

6. What are the qualifications of the CTA(s)?

7. How long has the current CTA(s) managed the fund?

8. What have been the total returns for the past one, three, five and ten years?

9. What is the fund's net asset value?

10. What is the fund's offering price?

✎ Grasping Managed Futures (Continued)

Your Portfolio Investment Questions (PIQs)

Name of investment _____ Date _____

11. What sales charges or fees will I incur if I buy or sell the units?

12. What are the management fees, brokerage fees and incentive fees?

13. What is the fund's current cash distribution?

14. What is the fund's break-even point?

15. What has been the range of the NAV for the past one, three, five and ten years, if applicable?

16. What types of economic scenarios could cause the fund's net asset value to increase?

17. What is my potential gain if I purchase the fund?

18. What types of economic scenarios could cause the fund's net asset value to decrease?

19. What is my potential loss if I purchase the fund?

Notes

CHAPTER 23

Introducing Managed Money Accounts

Even if you are not a multimillion dollar institution, you can be treated like one! Approximately 20,000 registered investment advisers manage money in the United States.

For many years, institutional investors, such as corporations, pension plans, universities and foundations have used professional money managers to invest their assets. Professional *money managers,* also known as *registered investment advisers* or *investment counselors,* are registered with the Securities and Exchange Commission (SEC).

Typically a *managed money account* is a method whereby an individual hires a registered investment adviser to trade (buy and sell) securities on his or her behalf based on a stated investment objective. The adviser has a defined investment style for managing the account. You too can obtain a money manager's professional services by establishing managed money accounts. Managed money accounts can be used for your *serious* or *investment money,* depending on the investment style and types of securities purchased.

Benefits of Using a Managed Money Account

When you establish a managed money account, you receive many benefits: (1) a portfolio of individual securities; (2) diversification; (3) professional portfolio management; (4) a stated investment style and discipline; (5) performance reports; (6) reasonable cost and (7) no decisions about when to buy or sell securities.

Additionally, you usually have an investment consultant who monitors your account, reviews the manager's performance and discusses market conditions with you on a regular basis.

Using a Managed Money Account

When you consider opening a managed money account, you need to obtain five services: (1) First you need an investment consultant to help you select a money manager; (2) then you need a money manager to manage the portfolio; (3) enter and execute orders; (4) retain custody of the assets; and (5) provide performance reports.

Selecting a Money Manager

Investment consultants are professionals who help you search for and select one or more money managers. Investment consulting firms specialize in this process and are paid a fee for their services. However, during the past 15 to 20 years, brokerage firms have offered individual investors the same investment consulting service through their own investment consulting services departments. These brokers who specialize in investment consulting know the styles of many money managers. After asking the appropriate questions regarding your investment objectives, risk tolerance and time horizon for investing, a consultant will recommend one or more money managers. Many brokerage and consulting firms use a computerized system to select the appropriate money manager for you.

Generally, the recommended money manager is independent of the brokerage or consultant's firm. However, many brokerage firms today also have their own divisions specializing in money management.

Each money manager is required to complete and file Form ADV, Parts I and II, with the SEC. Part II is available for your review and includes information about advisory services and fees, types of investments, methods of analysis, the management's education and business background. You may find it worthwhile to review Form ADV, Part II, before hiring a money manager.

How Money Managers Manage Money

Because you have specific investment objectives, it is of the utmost importance that you know the money manager's style or discipline (as discussed below). You want to be certain that the money manager suits your needs.

Managing Stock Portfolios

Money managers use specific investment styles or disciplines to invest the assets under their management. Some of the more common styles for stock selection are (1) contrarian, (2) growth, (3) long-term growth, (4) market-oriented, (5) market timing, (6) value and (7) yield. Following are brief explanations of each to acquaint you with the terminology.

Contrarian. With the *contrarian* method, when almost everyone sells, the contrarian manager buys; when almost everyone buys, the contrarian sells. For example, the contrarian buys a stock when the general outlook is unfavorable or sells a stock when the general outlook is favorable.

Growth. The *growth-oriented* manager looks for stocks that are expected to increase in value substantially during the near future. Typically, growth companies are forecasting to have high earnings growth and do not pay significant dividends. Growth stocks may be volatile.

Long-Term Growth. The *long-term growth* manager buys stocks that are expected to increase in value steadily over time, but not quite as quickly as growth stocks. Many long-term growth companies are forecasting to have steady earnings growth and pay dividends.

Market-Oriented. A manager who uses a *market-oriented* approach selects stocks that represent the overall market. Generally, the stocks are high quality, dividend paying and well known.

Market Timing. *Market timers* trade the market based on certain types of analysis. They generally use economic or company indicators to decide when to buy and sell. The investment manager may hold a stock for a short period of time or a long period of time, waiting for the appropriate sell signal. Furthermore, the market timer may hold cash reserves, waiting for the appropriate buy signal.

Value. *Value* managers analyze companies to find stocks selling near or below the value of the companies' assets, which is commonly known as *book value*. Many value stocks may be out of favor due to the condition of their industries or the economic outlook. Sometimes value stocks offer good dividends with relatively low price-earnings ratios.

Yield. Investment managers who use the *yield* method buy stocks based on their current dividend returns. Income return is important while the manager waits for the stock to increase in value. Many yield stocks are similar to value stocks since they also usually have low price-earnings ratios.

Types of Analysis for Making Selections

Money managers use different processes to decide which stocks to buy. Basically, two well-known processes help them make the final selection—top down and bottom up.

Top Down. *Top down* analysis begins with an overview of the economy. The portfolio manager evaluates the current economic condition, the economic outlook, the interest rate environment and any other economic or political events that may affect the markets. Next, the manager researches different industries to determine which ones may do well based on the previous analysis. From these industries, the manager evaluates individual companies to find the stocks selling for the best value.

Bottom Up. *Bottom up* analysis, considered the true stock selection process, reverses the order of top down analysis. It evaluates individual stocks first, then analyzes the respective industry, then assesses the economic environment.

Managing Bond Portfolios

Money managers use several styles when managing bonds, such as laddering, barbell, interest rate anticipation and interest rate reaction.

Laddering. The concept of *laddering* bonds is discussed in Financial Focus 4, "Laddering Securities."

Barbell. The *barbell* method creates a portfolio of both short-term notes, such as two to five years in maturity, and long-term notes, such as eight to ten years. Thus, the portfolio is overweighted in the short term and long term with no bonds maturing in between.

Interest Rate Anticipation. Bond managers use *interest rate anticipation* when they analyze various economic and market indicators to determine possible interest rate movements. They buy short-term, intermediate-term or long-term notes and bonds based on their anticipation of interest rate movements.

Interest Rate Reaction. Some managers believe that they cannot predict interest rates. Therefore, they buy and sell notes and bonds in *reaction* to changes in interest rates. They typically extend maturities when interest rates rise and shorten maturities when interest rates decline.

Entering and Executing Orders

Most money managers trade with discretion when placing orders in their clients' accounts. *Discretionary trading* means that your money manager does not get your approval before entering a trade. However, the brokerage firm you designate to execute orders sends a trade confirmation to you the next business day. This confirmation shows the appropriate information relating to the trade. You usually receive a monthly or quarterly statement from the money manager and brokerage firm showing all activity in the account.

Holding Custody of the Assets

Money managers do not hold securities; therefore, brokerage firms or bank trust departments must hold and safekeep the securities.

Providing Performance Reports

Your brokerage firm or money manager typically provides you with quarterly reports showing how your account has performed in absolute terms and relative to the popular market averages and indexes. (Refer to Financial Focus 9 for an explanation of market indexes.) The reports are quite comprehensive, detailing the securities bought and sold, the classification of securities, realized and unrealized gains and losses, percentage returns and income received.

Types of Accounts

Types of managed money accounts can vary as much as types of securities. The most common ones are (1) stocks, (2) international stocks, (3) government bonds, (4) municipal bonds, (5) international bonds and (6) balanced stocks and bonds. The risks and returns are different for each type of account. See Financial Focus 10 for a further explanation of risk and return.

Opening an Account

Each money manager sets a minimum account size. Normally, if a client hires the manager directly, the minimum may be $1 million or more. If the client hires a money manager through a brokerage firm, the minimum is often lowered to $100,000. To establish a managed money account, you sign papers to hire the manager, authorize discretionary trading, direct the orders through the broker and set the fees to be paid to the money manager and broker for designated services. An account may be terminated by either party with a written notice. Each account is separate and is not commingled with other accounts or securities.

Paying for Investment Services

You have several ways to pay for the managed money account services: (1) wrap fee accounts, (2) directed brokerage accounts and (3) fee brokerage accounts.

Wrap Fee Accounts. One common way to pay for the five services described above is with one inclusive annual fee known as a *wrap fee.* The annual fee is based on the value of the assets and is billed quarterly. The benefits of a wrap account are (1) all trades are executed without a commission; (2) you know the cost of maintaining the account each year; (3) the fee may be tax-deductible; and (4) the fee may be less expensive than if each service were being charged for separately.

Directed Brokerage Accounts. Another common way to pay for the five services is to remit to the money manager an annual fee based on the value of the assets in the account and to remit to the broker commissions for executing trades. These brokerage commissions also pay for the other services.

Fee Brokerage Accounts. Another way to pay for managed money account services is to remit to the manager and the brokerage firm separate fees, based on the value of the assets in the account. The fee you pay to the brokerage firm also covers the other services; thus, you are not charged any commissions for trading.

Your Portfolio Investment Questions (PIQs)

The number of money managers in the world is like the number of mutual funds: numerous. The key to selecting the appropriate money manager for you is to know their investment style and investment objective. You should narrow your list to three to five money managers by working with your investment consultant. The following PIQs should help you learn more about both of these criteria.

INVESTOR'S TIPS

PROCESS OF ESTABLISHING A MANAGED MONEY ACCOUNT

> Define your investment objective.

> Search for and evaluate the management firm that matches your investment objective.

> Understand the investment management style, types of securities and past performance.

> Select the investment management firm.

> Establish a brokerage account and a managed money account.

> Portfolio management

> Portfolio review and performance evaluation

Note: Your investment professional or consultant will help you with this process.

Introducing Managed Money Accounts

Your Portfolio Investment Questions (PIQs)

Name of money manager _____**Date** _____

1. How may I obtain a current ADV, Part II, report and brochure?

    Name   _____

    Firm   _____

    Address _____ Telephone number _____

            _____ Fax number   _____

2. How long has the firm been in business?

3. How many portfolio managers does the firm employ?

4. How much in assets does the firm manage?

5. What is the money manager's investment objective? (Check one.)

    _____ Long-term growth   _____ Growth

    _____ Growth and income   _____ Income and growth

    _____ Taxable income   _____ Tax-exempt income

6. What types of securities will the money manager purchase? (Check the appropriate ones.)

    _____ U.S. stocks   _____ Government notes and bonds

    _____ International stocks   _____ Municipal notes and bonds

    _____ Global stocks   _____ Corporate notes and bonds

    _____ Stocks and taxable bonds   _____ International notes and bonds

    _____ Stocks and tax-exempt bonds   _____ Other _____

Introducing Managed Money Accounts (Continued)

Your Portfolio Investment Questions (PIQs)

Name of money manager _____ **Date** _____

7. For a stock portfolio account, what is the money manager's investment style or discipline? (Check the appropriate ones.)

_____ Value   _____ Growth

_____ Market timing   _____ Market-oriented

_____ Yield   _____ Contrarian

_____ Long-term growth   _____ Other _____

_____ Bottom up   _____ Top down

8. For a bond portfolio account, what is the money manager's investment style or discipline? (Check the appropriate ones.)

_____ Interest rate reaction   _____ Interest rate anticipation

_____ Laddering maturities   _____ Other _____

_____ Barbell

9. What is the money manager's criteria for purchasing a security?

10. What is the money manager's criteria for selling a security?

11. What is the fee arrangement? (Check one.)

_____ Wrap fee account—one inclusive annual fee

_____ Directed brokerage account—annual management fee plus commissions

_____ Fee brokerage account—annual management fee plus brokerage fee

12. When are the fees charged?

13. How are the fees calculated?

✏ Introducing Managed Money Accounts (Continued)

Your Portfolio Investment Questions (PIQs)

Name of money manager _____ **Date** _____

14. Are any termination fees charged? If so, how?

15. What are the manager's performance returns for the past one, three, five and ten years? (Note: Performance return is *not* the most important criterion for a money manager. The investment style and discipline should meet your investment objective.)

16. What is the relative risk associated with the manager's returns?

17. What is your time horizon for investing (the average market cycle is three to five years)?

   _____ One to two years

   _____ Three to five years

   _____ Six to ten years

Notes

Appendix A
Financial Focuses

Financial Focus 1—Calculating Returns

Knowing your investment return is always a good idea. Calculating it is another one. Following are equations for various returns. The equations may seem a little complicated at first, but read them carefully and they will make sense. Usually your investment professional has quick access to these calculations.

Stocks

Current Yield. Use the following to calculate the current yield (CY) at this particular time:

Example: XYZ Corporation common stock is priced at $20 per share and pays an annual dividend of $1.

$$\frac{\$1 \text{ Annual dividend}}{\$20 \text{ Current market price}} \times 100 = 5\% \text{ CY}$$

When the stock price increases and the dividend remains the same, the CY decreases. When the stock price decreases and the dividend remains the same, the CY increases. While you own the stock, *your income is the dividend paid to you,* even though the CY changes due to stock price fluctuation. The CY calculation gives you only your percentage income return at a particular point in time, not your capital gain or loss. If you use the price you paid as the denominator, the result is the yield on your cost.

Bonds

Current Yield. Use the following to calculate the current yield (CY) at this particular time:

Example: U.S. Treasury bond 8% due 10/01/16 pays annual interest of $80 per $1,000 bond. Assume the bond is priced at a discount of 95 ($950) as of 10/01/96.

$$\frac{\$80 \text{ Annual interest}}{\$950 \text{ Current market price}} \times 100 = 8.42\% \text{ CY}$$

Yield to Maturity. The calculation for yield to maturity (percentage total return) is too complicated to explain here in detail. The yield to maturity (YTM) takes into account capital gain or loss, purchase price, redemption value, time to maturity and time between interest and all scheduled payments of interest and principal. Recognizing the time value of money, YTM is the discount rate at which the present value of all future payments would equal the present price of the bond. The calculation implicitly assumes that coupons are reinvested at the yield to maturity rate. Therefore, calculators or computers are used to figure the percentage. However, you can use a rule of thumb method that approximates the correct yield to maturity.

Use the following equation to calculate the approximate YTM for the previously mentioned bond priced at a *discount* of 95 ($950) at this particular time, assuming the bond is held to maturity:

$$\frac{\text{Annual interest} + [(\$1,000 - \text{Bond price}) \div \text{Years to maturity}]}{\frac{\text{Current market price} + \$1,000}{2}} \times 100 = \text{YTM}$$

or

$$\frac{\$80 + [(\$1,000 - \$950) \div 20]}{\frac{\$950 + \$1,000}{2}} \times 100 = 8.46\% \text{ YTM}$$

This formula is used to calculate the YTM of a premium bond, i.e., a bond whose market value is higher than the par value.

Note:

- The YTM for a bond priced at a discount is *greater* than the current yield.
- The YTM for a bond priced at a premium is *less* than the current yield.
- The YTM is *more important* than the current yield when buying a *premium bond.*

Yield to Call. Similar equations are used to calculate yield to call as are those used for yield to maturity *except* that the principal value at maturity is replaced by the first call price and the maturity date is replaced by the first call date. Assuming the bond issuer puts the company's well-being before the investor's well-being and calls the bonds if it is favorable to do so, the lesser of the yield to call and the yield to maturity is the more realistic rate of return to you.

Closed-End Funds

Distribution Rate. Typically, closed-end funds use the term *distribution rate* (also called *current yield*) to state the current return. The distribution rate is normally calculated by annualizing the latest dividend paid, then dividing it by the closing bid price. Use the following to calculate the distribution rate (current yield) at this particular time:

Example: XYZ Bond Fund pays a monthly dividend of $.06, and the current bid price is $10 per share.

$$\frac{(\$.06 \times 12) = \text{Annualized dividend}}{\$10 \text{ Current bid price}} \times 100 = 7.2\% \text{ Distribution rate/Current yield}$$

When the fund's price increases and the dividend remains the same, the current distribution rate decreases. When the fund's price decreases and the dividend remains the same, the current distribution rate increases. While you own the fund, *your income is the dividend paid to you,* even though the distribution rate changes due to the fund's price fluctuating. The distribution rate gives you only your percentage income return at a particular point in time, not your capital gain or loss.

Open-End Funds (Mutual Funds)

In 1988, the Securities and Exchange Commission (SEC) adopted a standardized yield formula (the *SEC yield*) to establish a uniform basis for advertising the income performance of open-end funds (mutual funds). The purpose of the SEC yield is to increase the investor's ability to compare and evaluate the income performance regardless of how a fund distributes its net investment income. The SEC yield is determined on a yield to maturity basis, whereas the fund's distribution rate is based on the actual distributions made to shareholders.

Also, the SEC has adopted a standardized total return to establish a uniform basis for calculating returns.

SEC Yield. The SEC yield formula uses an approximate, theoretical current income derived from the portfolio of securities after expenses. The income is calculated over a 30-day base period and divided by the current offering price. This figure is compounded monthly for six months and then annualized. The resulting percentage is the SEC yield. The formula does not include any realized gains from portfolio transactions.

Distribution Rate. The distribution rate formula uses the current net investment income paid to you. This figure is then annualized and divided by the fund's current offering price. The distribution paid may include short-term capital gains, which may or may not occur in the future.

Standardized SEC Total Return. Because the SEC yield and the distribution rate often differ, a better calculation may be the total return of the fund. The calculation for total return uses both income received (or reinvested) and capital appreciation or loss over a period of specified years.

Total return is the figure you need most to review and analyze the fund's performance. This figure tells you whether your investment is making money or losing money after all income earned and capital appreciation or depreciation.

Unit Investment Trusts

Unit investment trusts usually use two methods to figure income return: (1) estimated current return and (2) estimated long-term return.

Estimated Current Return. Estimated current return shows the estimated annual cash to be received by the unit holder (net of estimated annual expenses) divided by the public offering price.

Estimated Long-Term Return. The estimated long-term return is a measure of the estimated return over the UIT's life. The return represents an average of the yields to maturity (or call date) of the individual bonds in the portfolio.

Read the prospectus for each *different* unit investment trust for further explanation of how yields and returns are calculated.

Financial Focus 2—Why Diversify?

If you could predict the future, you would not need to diversify. You would always buy the best performing investment and never worry that you could lose money. In reality, because some investments will provide you with significant returns while others will serve up capital losses, diversifying enables you to try to achieve an overall good return from several investments.

The following two tables compare investment in a single asset versus investment in five different ones. Figure A.1 illustrates the total profit from a single investment earning a 6 percent compounded annual rate of return for 15 years. Figure A.2 illustrates the total profit from five different investments earning different returns, ranging from losing all of the investment to earning a 15 percent compounded annual rate of return for 15 years.

FIGURE A.1   One $25,000 Investment—15-Year Period

Investment Alternative	Amount Invested	Compounded Annual Return	Ending Value	Total Profit
A	$25,000	6%	$59,913.50	$34,913.50

FIGURE A.2   Five $5,000 Investments—15-Year Period

Investment Alternative	Amount Invested	Compounded Annual Return	Ending Value	Total Profit
A	$ 5,000	Investment lost	$ 0.00	($5,000.00)
B	5,000	0%	5,000.00	0.00
C	5,000	6	11,982.70	6,982.70
D	5,000	10	20,886.20	15,886.20
E	5,000	15	40,685.20	35,685.20
Total	$25,000		$78,554.10	$53,554.10

As you can see, the single $25,000 investment resulted in a $34,913.50 profit, while the five investments totaling $25,000 resulted in a $53,554.10 gain, or an additional profit of $18,640.60. The money that was diversified among five different investments had a better overall return than the single investment even though one entire investment was lost.

Of course, the results would be different had all the investments performed with higher or lower rates of return. The point is that you may achieve a better return when you diversify than when you invest in a single investment.

Financial Focus 3—Portfolio Models

Portfolio Model I

You can structure your portfolio in so many different ways. A basic portfolio approach is to allocate your assets among three categories, such as money market funds, bonds and stocks. The percentage placed in each category is based on your age. As you grow older, the percentages change. Figure A.3 displays the allocation of assets for the different age groups.

FIGURE A.3   A Portfolio Model Based on Age

Age	Stocks	Bonds and Money Market Securities
25	75%	25%
30	70	30
35	65	35
40	60	40
45	55	45
50	50	50
55	45	55
60	40	60
65	35	65
70	30	70
75	25	75
80	20	80

The diversification within each category is based on your investment objective. Investing in high-quality stocks for the long term is a good idea. Also, your tax bracket may determine whether you purchase municipal, government or corporate bonds. Once again, staying with high-quality bonds and notes is usually a sound portfolio decision. You may purchase stocks and bonds by investing in individual securities, mutual funds, closed-end funds, UITs and variable annuities.

Portfolio Model II

A second method for developing a portfolio is another allocation of assets approach using six asset categories. The allocation, as shown in Figure A.4, is based upon such factors as your age, financial condition, health, investment objective and risk tolerance. The only assumption is that the primary investment objective is *capital appreciation (growth)*.

FIGURE A.4   A Portfolio Model Based on Various Factors

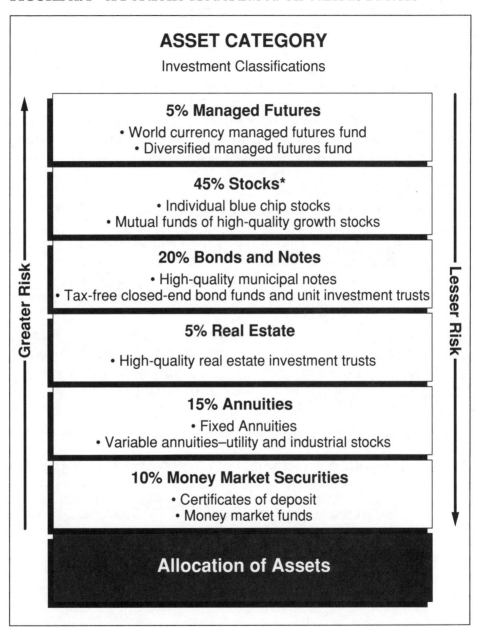

ASSET CATEGORY
Investment Classifications

5% Managed Futures
- World currency managed futures fund
- Diversified managed futures fund

45% Stocks*
- Individual blue chip stocks
- Mutual funds of high-quality growth stocks

20% Bonds and Notes
- High-quality municipal notes
- Tax-free closed-end bond funds and unit investment trusts

5% Real Estate
- High-quality real estate investment trusts

15% Annuities
- Fixed Annuities
- Variable annuities–utility and industrial stocks

10% Money Market Securities
- Certificates of deposit
- Money market funds

Allocation of Assets

Greater Risk → / Lesser Risk →

*Stocks should be diversified primarily in the U.S. markets, with some invested internationally.

Financial Focus 4—Laddering Securities

Because changes in interest rates are very difficult to predict, you may not know whether to buy long-term CDs and bonds or short-term CDs and notes. An effective method used to manage money and help solve this problem is the *ladder portfolio* approach. Most investors use CDs, U.S. Treasury securities or zero-coupon bonds to ladder, although other securities with fixed maturity dates may also be used.

Strategy of Laddering Maturity Dates

Instead of buying one particular maturity date, you might buy securities across several maturity dates. For example, you may want to buy maturities from one to three years, or from one to five years, or even from one to ten years. Use approximately the same dollar amount for each maturity.

Figure A.5 shows a hypothetical five-year CD ladder portfolio. Its strategy is simple. As the first CD matures, you buy another CD with a five-year maturity. Your ladder is still one through five years. As the next CD matures, you buy another five-year CD. You continue to buy a five-year CD as each CD matures.

FIGURE A.5   Example of a Five-Year CD Ladder Portfolio

Investment Amount	Security Purchased	Percent Yield (APY)	Maturity Date
$ 5,000	CD	5.00	1 Year
5,000	CD	5.50	2 Year
5,000	CD	6.00	3 Year
5,000	CD	6.50	4 Year
5,000	CD	7.00	5 Year
$25,000	Average Yield:	6.00	

Benefits of Laddering Securities

Longer term maturities typically offer greater yields than shorter term maturities. Therefore, when you buy a long-term security with the greater yield, you increase your income for that year. This procedure reduces your *reinvestment risk,* which is the risk of having to reinvest your maturing principal at lower interest rates.

In the hypothetical ladder, if interest rates increased when you rolled over your first CD, the longer term CD would generally provide a greater yield than the one maturing. If interest rates decreased when you rolled over your first CD, at least you would have locked in higher yields when you purchased the longer term maturities. Thus, you would have averaged the interest rates over the period of the ladder.

Of course, this approach also offers liquidity because you have a CD maturing each year. Any dollar amount and any time interval, such as every 3, 6, 12 or 24 months, may be used when you ladder securities.

Financial Focus 5—Comparing Taxable Yields to Tax-Exempt Yields

---

Taxable-Equivalent Yield

It is important to compare tax-exempt income to taxable income to determine which is better for you. To compare these figures, calculate the taxable-equivalent yield for a tax-exempt yield. The formula is as follows:

$$\frac{\text{Tax-exempt yield}}{(1 - \text{Tax bracket})} = \text{Taxable-equivalent yield}$$

Example: If you are in a 28% tax bracket and receive a 6.00% tax-exempt yield, the taxable-equivalent yield is calculated as follows:

$$\frac{6\% \text{ Tax-exempt yield}}{(1 - 0.28 \text{ Tax bracket})} = \frac{6\%}{.72} = 8.33\% \text{ Taxable-equivalent yield}$$

To double-check your calculation from the previous example, use the following method:

8.33%	Taxable yield
× .28	Tax bracket
2.33%	Taxable amount

8.33%	Taxable yield
− 2.33	Taxable amount
6.00%	After-tax yield

Therefore, the 6 percent tax-exempt yield is equivalent to an 8.33 percent taxable yield. In this case, if you receive a taxable yield greater than 8.33 percent on a comparable investment of the same quality or maturity date, it may be better to purchase the taxable investment. However, if the taxable investment is lower quality, the comparison based solely on yields is not valid.

If your state or city has an income tax, the tax bracket figure should include the sum of the federal, state and city income tax rates.

Figure A.6 displays the taxable-equivalent yields for selected tax-exempt yields. To use the chart, select your tax bracket on the left side of the table, then move across the line to the appropriate column for the tax-exempt yield. The number where the row and column intersect is the taxable-equivalent yield.

FIGURE A.6   Tax-Equivalent Yield Chart

Tax Bracket	4.00%	4.50%	5.00%	5.50%	6.00%	6.50%	7.00%
15.0%	4.71	5.29	5.88	6.47	7.05	7.65	8.24
28.0%	5.55	6.25	6.94	7.63	8.33	9.03	9.72
31.0%	5.80	6.52	7.25	7.97	8.7	9.42	10.14
36.0%	6.25	7.03	7.81	8.59	9.38	10.16	10.94
39.6%	6.62	7.45	8.28	9.1	9.93	10.76	11.59

Financial Focus 6—Why Bond Prices Change

One of the hardest concepts to understand is why bond and note prices change. Two basic features that most bonds and notes have are (1) a fixed interest rate (coupon rate) and (2) a fixed maturity date. Existing bonds in the secondary marketplace "compete" with newly issued bonds in respect to both current yield and yield to maturity. As new bonds are issued during times of fluctuating interest rates, the only thing that can change on an existing bond to compete with the new bonds is the *market price.* Consequently, the changing market price provides revised yields, which can now compete with the new bonds' yields.

Example: Today you buy a $1,000 U.S. Treasury bond 9% due 10/01/16 for 100 ($1,000). Your cost is $1,000, and you receive income of $90 per year until 10/01/16. Therefore, your current yield today is 9% ($90 ÷ $1,000 × 100).

One month later the Federal Reserve Bank raises interest rates and the federal government issues a new bond, such as a U.S. Treasury bond 10 percent due 11/01/16 at 100 ($1,000). If you want to sell your 9% bond, how much is it worth in the marketplace?

An investor could buy the new 10% bond and receive $100 per year until 11/01/16 (a 10% current yield), or the investor could buy your 9% bond depending on the market price. For the investor to receive a 10% current yield from your bond, he or she would pay you $900 ($90 income ÷ 10% current yield). Thus, the investor could either buy your bond for $900 and receive $90 or buy the new bond for $1,000 and receive $100. Either way, the investor has the opportunity to earn a 10% current yield. *As you can see, as interest rates rise, bond prices decrease.*

In this example, the 1% change of interest rate in one month is for illustration purposes only. Also, the level of yields to maturity for other bonds may affect the market price and cause your bond to trade for more or less than $900.

Furthermore, as interest rates fall, bond prices increase.

Financial Focus 7—Viewing the Yield Curve

Interest rates, which affect market values of debt securities prior to maturity, are constantly changing based on such factors as inflation and the state of the economy. Each market segment—government, municipal and corporate bond markets—generally offers different interest rates or yields in relation to changing economic and market events. One of the best ways to analyze interest rates is to plot a yield curve. The *yield curve* shows the current picture of interest rates for a particular market sector in graphic form. The horizontal axis of the graph represents the maturity of the security being plotted, which generally ranges between six months to 30 years. The vertical axis of the graph represents interest rate or yield of each security based on its maturity. The general rule of thumb regarding yields and maturities is that the longer the maturity, the higher the yield of the debt security. The benefit of a yield curve is that it can help you determine how far out in time you may need to invest to obtain a certain yield. Typically, the point where the yield curve is the steepest is where you can receive the most return for the least amount of risk. Figure A.7 shows an example of a yield curve. The example is considered a *normal yield curve* because it shows higher yields for longer maturities. An *inverted yield curve* would reflect the opposite with shorter-term maturities providing high yields than longer-term maturities. A *flat yield curve* occurs when short-term and long-term maturities provide approximately the same level of yield. In this case, investors generally stay short term because that can capture the same yields without adding risk to their portfolios.

FIGURE A.7   A Sample Yield Curve

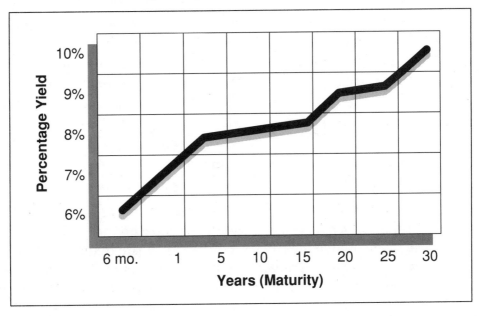

Financial Focus 8—Listing Cash Dividend Dates

Cash Dividend Dates

You can use four dividend dates to help you understand who is entitled to the cash dividend when it is declared by the corporation's board of directors: (1) declaration date; (2) record date; (3) payable date; and (4) ex-dividend date.

The company paying the cash dividend sets the first three dates. The marketplace where the stock trades determines the fourth date.

The *declaration date* is the date the company announces the (1) payment of a cash dividend, (2) the cut-off date for shareholders of record and (3) the date payment is to be made.

The *record date* is the cut-off date for shareholders to receive the dividend. You must own stock as of this date to receive the dividend.

FIGURE A.8   Example of Cash Dividend Dates

Declaration date	Tuesday, March 4th	Company declares dividend, record date and payable date
Ex-dividend date	Thursday, March 11th	Two business days before the record date
Record date	Monday, March 15th	Cut-off for owners to receive dividend
Payable date	Wednesday, April 1st	Shareholders receive dividend

The *payable date* is the date the company sends the dividend check. As long as you were the owner on the record date, you do not have to own the stock on the payable date to receive the check.

The *ex-dividend date* is the date when a buyer of the stock is not entitled to the dividend. If you buy the stock ex-dividend, you will not receive the current dividend.

Regular way stock transactions settle in three business days (i.e., three business days after the trade date). Therefore, legal ownership occurs on the settlement date. Of course, you are committed to the purchase transacted on the trade date and obligated to pay the brokerage firm by the settlement date. If you sell the stock on the ex-dividend date, you are entitled to that dividend on the payable date. This is because you are still the owner as of the record date (the transaction doesn't settle until three business days after the trade date).

Figure A.8 provides an example of the dividend dates for a regular way transaction.

Financial Focus 9—Market Indexes

Many indexes are used to evaluate returns for the performance of the stock and bond markets. You can also compare your portfolio returns to these indexes. The type of portfolio and investment objective determine which index is appropriate for comparison. Below are some of the important indexes you might use:

- The *Dow Jones Industrial Average (DJIA)* is an average of the stock prices of 30 major industrial companies. The average is quoted in points, not dollars.
- The *Standard & Poor's 500 Index (S&P 500)* is an index of 500 industrial, financial, utility and transportation stocks. The index is quoted in points, not dollars.
- The *New York Stock Exchange Composite Index* is an index of every common stock traded on the New York Stock Exchange. The index is quoted in points, not dollars.
- The *Nasdaq Index* is an index of about 4,500 domestic over-the-counter (OTC) stocks. The index is quoted in points, not dollars.
- The *Nasdaq 100 Index* is an index of the 100 largest domestic OTC stocks. The index is quoted in points, not dollars.
- The *Lehman Brothers Government/Corporate Intermediate Bond Index* is an index composed of investment-grade corporate and government bonds of large issuers ($100 million or more) with maturities between 1 and 9.99 years.
- The *Lehman Brothers Government/Corporate Long-Term Bond Index* is an index composed of investment-grade corporate and government bonds of large issuers ($100 million or more) with maturities of 10 years or longer.
- The *Morgan Stanley Capital International Europe, Australia, Far East (EAFE) Index* is an index of approximately 900 stocks listed on exchanges in Australia, Austria, Belgium, Denmark, Finland, France, Germany, Hong Kong, Italy, Japan, Malaysia, the Netherlands, New Zealand, Norway, Singapore, Spain, Sweden, Switzerland and the United Kingdom.

Financial Focus 10—Plotting Risk and Return

Every type of investment can be plotted on a chart showing its rate of return and its risk. The rate of return (reward) figure can represent any number of years, such as one, three, five, ten or more. The rate of return is the total return, i.e., capital gain or loss plus income earned. The risk is the standard deviation of the return. *Standard deviation* is the variation of the return compared to the average or expected return. In simple terms, it is a measure of volatility of the investment's performance. In theory, the greater the investment risk, the greater the *potential* for a larger return.

Normally, you want an investment that has the greatest return with the least risk. One of the best ways to analyze investments or investment managers is to plot on a graph their returns and the risk associated with achieving these returns. Typically, those investments or investment managers who appear in the upper left corner of the graph, known as the *northwest quadrant,* provide the *possibility* of the greatest returns with the least risk. Investment consultants and money managers usually use this type of chart to show risk and returns. Plotting various asset categories by this method is one way to analyze the potential risk and returns for different allocation percentages of various asset categories. Figure A.9 shows the four quadrants of risk and rates of return.

Selecting a Money Manager

When selecting a money manager, try to find one whose returns fall in the upper left corner of the chart, the northwest quadrant. A money manager who earns high returns with low risk offers you a good management style. A money manager whose returns fall in the upper right corner, known as the *northeast quadrant,* may provide high returns, but even higher risk and volatility. When selecting a money manager, you also want to know what types of securities he or she will purchase and the manager's investment style. Your investment objective will determine which type of manager suits you. Of course, past

FIGURE A.9   Quadrants of Risk and Rates of Return

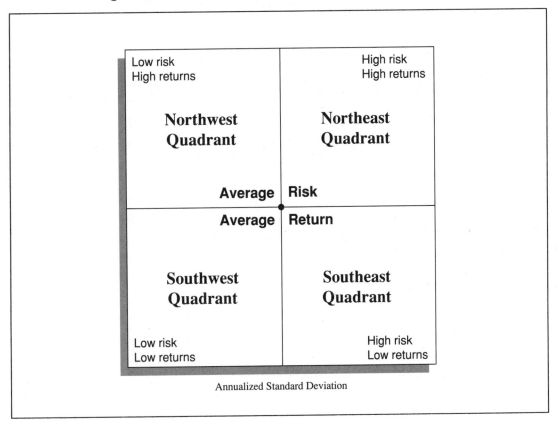

Low risk
High returns

High risk
High returns

**Northwest
Quadrant**

**Northeast
Quadrant**

Average | Risk

Average | Return

**Southwest
Quadrant**

**Southeast
Quadrant**

Low risk
Low returns

High risk
Low returns

Annualized Standard Deviation

results do not indicate future performance. The money manager may attempt to achieve higher returns with less risk, but may actually achieve lower returns and higher risk.

Selecting Mutual Funds

Mutual funds' performance returns may be plotted the same way as money managers' returns. Each mutual fund has a risk associated with its past performance. Like you would with any investment, review the kinds of securities the mutual fund purchases and the fund's investment style. "How much return do I expect for how much risk?" is the question you should always ask.

Appendix B

Tax Information Forms

Tax Information

Money Market Funds, Money Market Deposit Accounts and Certificates of Deposit (CDs)

Money Market Funds and Money Market Deposit Accounts
Purchase Information (Complete where applicable.)

Account registration _____ Account # _____

Fund/account name _____

Investment professional _____

Firm established through _____

Address _____

_____

Telephone number_____ Fax _____

CUSIP number_____ Symbol _____

Purchase date_____Amount $ _____

Certificates of Deposit (CDs)
Purchase information (Complete where applicable.)

Account registration _____ Account # _____

Issuer's name_____

Investment professional _____

Firm purchased through_____

Address _____

_____

Telephone number_____ Fax _____

CUSIP number _____ Symbol _____

Purchase date_____ Amount $ _____

Interest payment dates_____

Maturity date_____ Interest reinvested? _____ Yes _____ No

Tax Information
Fixed Annuities and Variable Annuities

Fixed Annuities

Purchase Information (Complete where applicable.)

Account registration _____ Policy # _____

Insurance company_____

Insurance professional_____

Firm purchased through_____

Address _____

Telephone number_____ Fax _____

Name of owner _____ Annuitant _____

Name of beneficiary _____

Initial interest rate _____ % Number of years _____

Purchase date_____ Premium paid $ _____

Maturity date _____

Variable Annuities

Purchase Information (Complete where applicable.)

Account registration _____ Policy # _____

Insurance company_____

Insurance professional_____

Firm purchased through_____

Address _____

Telephone number _____ Fax _____

Name of owner _____ Annuitant _____

Name of beneficiary _____

Investment allocation	$ Amount	Account Type	Percentage
	$_____	_____	____ %
	$_____	_____	____ %
	$_____	_____	____ %
	$_____	_____	____ %

Tax Information
Immediate Annuities and Life Insurance

Immediate Annuities
Purchase Information (Complete where applicable.)

Account registration _____ Policy # _____

Insurance company_____

Insurance professional_____

Firm purchased through _____

Address _____

_____

Telephone number_____ Fax _____

Name of owner _____ Annuitant _____

Name of owner's beneficiary _____

Premium paid $_____

Payment period _____ Monthly _____ Quarterly _____ Annually

Payment option_____ Payment to be received $_____

Life Insurance
Purchase Information (Complete where applicable.)

Account registration _____ Policy # _____

Insurance company_____

Insurance professional_____

Firm purchased through _____

Address _____

_____

Telephone number_____ Fax _____

Name of owner_____ Insured _____

Name of beneficiary _____

Initial purchase date_____ Initial premium $ _____

Subsequent payments_____ Monthly _____ Quarterly _____ Annually

Subsequent premium $ _____ Death benefit $ _____

Tax Information

Bonds, Notes and Bills

Purchase Information (Complete where applicable.)

Account registration _____ Account # _____

Name of security _____

_____

Coupon interest rate_____ %   Maturity date _____

Investment professional _____

Firm purchased through_____

Address _____

_____

Telephone number_____ Fax _____

CUSIP number_____ Symbol _____

Marketplace for security_____

Trade date _____ Settlement date _____

Principal amount $ _____ Purchase price $_____

Total cost basis $ _____ Accrued interest paid $ _____
(Total cost basis excludes accrued interest paid.)

Interest payment dates_____

Subsequent Information

Record of company mergers, distributions or name changes

Date _____ Terms of distribution _____

Date _____ Terms of merger _____

Date _____ New name _____

Sale Information

Trade date _____ Settlement date _____

Principal amount $ _____ Sales price $ _____

Net proceeds $ _____ Accrued interest received $ _____
(Net proceeds equals principal value minus commission, if any; excludes accrued interest received.)

Profit or loss $_____
(Net proceeds minus total cost basis.)

Tax Information

Common Stocks and Preferred Stocks

Purchase Information (Complete where applicable.)

Account registration _____ Account # _____

Name of security _____

Type of stock_____

Investment professional _____

Firm purchased through _____

Address _____

_____

Telephone number_____ Fax _____

CUSIP number_____ Symbol _____

Marketplace for security _____

Trade date _____ Settlement date _____

Shares purchased_____

Purchase price $ _____ Total cost basis $ _____

Subsequent Information

Date dividend reinvestment plan established _____
(Retain all year-end statements.)

Stock splits/stock dividends   Year _____   Terms _____

Year _____   Terms _____

Year _____   Terms _____

Record of company mergers, distributions or name changes

Date _____   Terms of distribution _____

Date _____   Terms of merger _____

Date _____   New name _____

Sale Information

Trade date _____ Settlement date _____

Shares sold _____ Sales price $ _____

Net proceeds $ _____
(Net proceeds equals principal value minus commission.)

Profit or loss $ _____
(Net proceeds minus total cost basis.)

Tax Information

Open-End Funds (Mutual Funds), Closed-End Funds and Unit Investment Trusts (UITs)

Purchase Information (Complete where applicable.)

Account registration _____ Account # _____

Name of security _____

Type of fund/trust _____

Investment professional _____

Firm purchased through _____

Address _____

_____

Telephone number_____ Fax _____

CUSIP number _____ Symbol _____

Marketplace for security _____

Trade date _____ Settlement date _____

Shares/units purchased _____

Purchase price $_____ Total cost basis $ _____

Subsequent Information

Date dividend reinvestment plan established _____
(Retain all year-end statements.)

Stock splits/stock dividends   Year _____ Terms _____

                                        Year _____ Terms _____

                                        Year _____ Terms _____

Record of company mergers, distributions or name changes

Date _____ Terms of distribution _____

Date _____ Terms of merger _____

Date _____ New name _____

Sale Information

Trade date _____ Settlement date _____

Shares/units sold _____ Sales price $ _____

Net proceeds $ _____
(Net proceeds equals principal value minus commission.)

Profit or loss $ _____
(Net proceeds minus total cost basis.)

Tax Information

Limited Partnerships and Managed Futures Funds

Purchase Information (Complete where applicable.)

Account registration _____ Account # _____

Name of partnership/fund _____

Type of partnership/fund _____

Investment professional _____

Firm purchased through _____

Address _____

_____

Telephone number_____ Fax _____

CUSIP number _____ Symbol _____

Marketplace for partnership/fund_____

Trade date _____ Settlement date _____

Shares/units purchased _____

Purchase price $ _____ Total cost basis $ _____

Subsequent Information

Record of company mergers, distributions or name changes

Date _____Terms of distribution _____

Date _____Terms of merger _____

Date _____New name _____

Sale Information

Trade date _____ Settlement date _____

Shares/units sold _____ Sales price $ _____

Net proceeds $ _____
(Net proceeds equals principal value minus commission.)

Profit or loss $ _____
(Net proceeds minus total cost basis.)

Tax Information

Managed Money Accounts

Account Information (Complete where applicable.)

Account registration _____ Account # _____

Name of investment manager_____

Type of account_____
(Stocks, bonds, balanced)

Type of securities_____
(United States, international, global)

Investment objective _____

_____

Investment professional _____

Firm established through _____

Address _____

_____

Telephone number _____ Fax _____

Method of payment _____ Wrap fee *(inclusive management and brokerage fee)*

_____ Directed brokerage *(management fee plus commission)*

_____ Fee brokerage *(management fee plus brokerage fee)*

Inception value $ _____ Inception date _____

Amount added $ _____ Date _____

Amount added $ _____ Date _____

Amount withdrawn $ _____ Date _____

Amount withdrawn $ _____ Date _____

Appendix C
Resources

Industry Organizations

American Association of Individual Investors (AAII)
625 North Michigan Avenue, Suite 1900
Chicago, IL 60611

American Stock Exchange (AMEX)
86 Trinity Place
New York, NY 10006-1881

Commodity Futures Trading Commission (CFTC)
2033 K Street, N.W.
Washington, DC 20581

Federal Reserve Bank (FRB)
20th Street and C Street, N.W.
Washington, DC 20551

Federal Deposit Insurance Corporation (FDIC)
550 17th Street, N.W.
Washington, DC 20429

Investment Company Institute (ICI)
1401 H Street, N.W., Suite 1200
Washington, DC 20005-2148

Managed Futures Association (MFA)
P.O. Box 761
Palo Alto, CA 94302

Municipal Securities Rulemaking Board (MSRB)
1150 18th Street, N.W., Suite 400
Washington, DC 20036

National Association of Insurance Commissioners (NAIC)
444 North Capitol Street, N.W., Suite 309
Washington, DC 20001-1512

National Association of Securities Dealers, Inc. (NASD)
1735 K Street, N.W.
Washington, DC 20006-1506

New York Stock Exchange, Inc. (NYSE)
11 Wall Street
New York, NY 10005

Securities and Exchange Commission (SEC)
450 5th Street, N.W.
Washington, DC 20549

Securities Institute Association (SIA)
120 Broadway
New York, NY 10271-0080

Securities Investor Protection Corporation (SIPC)
805 Fifteenth Street, N.W., Suite 800
Washington, DC 20005-2207

Research Services Firms

A.M. Best Company
Ambest Road
Oldwick, NJ 08858

Daily Graphs, Inc.
Daily Graphs
P.O. Box 66919
Los Angeles, CA 90066

Dow Jones & Company
World Financial Center
200 Liberty Street
New York, NY 10281

Duff & Phelps Credit Rating Company
55 East Monroe Street, Suite 3500
Chicago, IL 60603

Federal Reserve Bank of St. Louis
U.S. Financial Data
P.O. Box 66953
St. Louis, MO 63166-6953

Ibbotson Associates
225 North Michigan Avenue, Suite 700
Chicago, IL 60601-7676

IBC/Donoghue, Inc.
Money Fund Report
P.O. Box 91004
Ashland, MA 01721-9104

Lipper Analytical Services, Inc.
47 Maple Street
Summit, NJ 07901

Mansfield Charts
2973 Kennedy Boulevard
Jersey City, NJ 07306

Moody's Investors Service, Inc.
99 Church Street
New York, NY 10007

Morningstar, Inc.
225 West Wacker Drive
Chicago, IL 60606

National Quotation Bureau, Inc.
150 Commerce Road
Cedar Grove, NJ 07009-1208

Securities Research Company
101 Prescott Street
Wellesley Hills, MA 02181-3319

Standard & Poor's Corporation
25 Broadway
New York, NY 10004

Value Line Publishing, Inc.
220 East 42nd Street
New York, NY 10017-5891

Newspapers

Barron's
Investor's Business Daily
The New York Times

USA TODAY
The Wall Street Journal

Magazines

Business Week
Changing Times
Financial World
Forbes
Fortune
Kiplinger's Personal Finance Magazine
Money
Worth

Newsletters

Dick Davis Digest
P.O. Box 350630
Ft. Lauderdale, FL 33335-0630

The Hulbert Financial Digest
Newsletter Directory
Mark Hulbert
316 Commerce Street
Alexandria, VA 22314

The Zweig Forecast
P.O. Box 2900
Wantagh, NY 11793

Books

The Annuity Handbook: A Guide to
Nonqualified Annuities
Darlene K. Chandler
The National Underwriter Company

The Basics of Bonds
Gerald Krefetz
Dearborn Financial Publishing, Inc.

Beating the Dow
Michael O'Higgins with John Downes
Harper Perennial

The Budget Kit: The Common Cent$ Money
Management Workbook
Judy Lawrence
Dearborn Financial Publishing, Inc.

The Finance and Investment Handbook
John Downes and Jordan E. Goodman
Barron's Educational Series

*The Income Investor: Choosing Investments
That Pay Cash Today and Tomorrow*
Donald R. Nichols
Dearborn Financial Publishing, Inc.

The Investor's Information Sourcebook
Spencer McGowan
New York Institute of Finance

The Life Insurance Kit
Terry R. O'Neill
Dearborn Financial Publishing, Inc.

*1995 Field Guide to Estate Planning, Business
Planning and Employee Benefits*
Donald F. Cody
The National Underwriter Company

One Up On Wall Street
Peter Lynch with John Rothchild
Simon & Schuster/Penguin Books

*The Wall Street Journal Guide To
Understanding Money and Investments*
Kenneth M. Morris and Alan M. Siegel
Lightbulb Press/Fireside/Simon & Schuster, Inc.

*The Wall Street Journal Guide To
Understanding Personal Finance*
Kenneth M. Morris and Alan M. Siegel
Lightbulb Press/Fireside/Simon & Schuster, Inc.

Martin Zweig's Winning on Wall Street
Martin Zweig
Warner Books

Computer Software Program

Quicken
Intuit Inc.
P.O. Box 3014
Menlo Park, CA 94026

Glossary

Special appreciation is extended to Dearborn's Securities Product Development for assisting me in compiling this glossary.

accrued interest   Interest that is added to the contract price of a bond transaction. This interest has accrued since the last interest payment up to but not including the settlement date. Exceptions are income bonds, bonds in default and zero-coupon bonds.

ADR   *See* American depositary receipt.

American depositary receipt (ADR)   A negotiable receipt for a given number of shares of stock in a foreign corporation. An ADR is bought and sold in the U.S. securities markets just as stock is traded.

ask   The current price for which a security may be bought, as in the OTC and NYSE markets. For mutual funds, the asked price includes any sales charge that is added to the net asset value. *See also* offer, public offering price. (*Syn.* offer, quotation, quote)

basis point   Equal to 1/100 of 1 percent of yield (e.g., ½ percent = 50 basis points).

bearer bond   *See* coupon bond.

bear market   A market in which prices of securities are falling or are expected to fall.

beta coefficient   A means of measuring the volatility of a security or portfolio of securities in comparison with the market as a whole. A beta of 1 indicates that the security's price will move with the market. A beta higher than 1 indicates that the security's price will be more volatile than the market. A beta of less than 1 means that the security will be less volatile than the market as a whole.

bid   An indication by an investor, a trader or a dealer of a willingness to buy a security or commodity. *See also* ask, offer. (*Syn.* quotation, quote)

bid price   *See* net asset value.

bond quote   A corporate bond that is quoted on a percentage of par with increments of ⅛, where a quote of 99⅛ represents 99.125 percent of par ($1,000), or $991.25. Bonds may also be quoted on a yield to maturity basis.

book-entry security   A security sold without delivery of a certificate. Evidence of ownership is maintained on records kept by a central agency, such as the Treasury on the sale of Treasury bills. Transfer of ownership is recorded by entering the change with the agency.

bull market   A market in which prices of securities are moving higher or are expected to move higher.

business day   A day on which the NYSE is open for business (trading).

callable bond   A type of bond issued with a provision allowing the issuer to redeem the bond prior to maturity at a predetermined price. *See also* call price.

callable preferred stock   A type of preferred stock carrying the provision that the corporation retains the right to call in the stock at a certain price and retire it. *See also* call price.

call date   The date after which the issuer of a bond has the option to redeem the issue at par or at par plus a premium.

call price   The price paid (usually a premium over the par value of the issue) for preferred stocks or bonds redeemed prior to maturity of the issue.

capital appreciation   A rise in the market prices of assets owned.

capital gain   The gain (selling price minus cost basis) on an asset. *See also* capital loss.

capitalization   The sum of a company's long-term debt, capital stock and surpluses. *See also* capital structure. (*Syn.* invested capital)

capital loss The loss (cost basis minus selling price) on an asset. *See also* capital gain.

capital market That segment of the securities market that deals in instruments with more than one year to maturity—that is, long-term debt and equity securities.

capital structure The composition of long-term funds (equity and debt) a company has as a source for financing. *See also* capitalization.

cash account An account in which a client is required by Regulation T to pay in full for securities purchased not later than the third business day from the trade date.

cash dividend A cash payment to a company's stockholders out of the company's current earnings or accumulated profits. The dividend must be declared by the board of directors.

cash equivalent A security that is extremely liquid and can be readily converted into cash.

chartist A securities analyst who uses charts and graphs of the past price movements of a security to predict its future movements. *See also* technical analysis.

commercial paper An unsecured, short-term promissory note issued by a corporation chiefly for financing accounts receivable. It is usually issued at a discount reflecting prevailing market interest rates. Maturities range up to 270 days.

common stock An equity security that represents ownership in a corporation. *See also* equity.

conversion ratio The number of shares per $1,000 debenture (or preferred stock) that the holder would receive if the debenture (or preferred stock) were converted into shares of common stock.

convertible bond A type of debt security (usually in the form of a debenture) that can be converted into (exchanged for) equity securities of the issuing corporation—that is, common and preferred stock.

cost-push inflation A type of inflation caused by higher production costs (e.g., wages).

coupon bond A bond without the name of the owner printed on its face and with coupons representing semiannual interest payments attached. Coupons are submitted to the trustee by the holder to receive the interest payments. (*Syn.* bearer bond)

custodian The institution or person responsible for protecting the property of another. Mutual funds have custodians responsible for safeguarding certificates and performing clerical duties. Also, someone who takes charge of an incompetent's affairs.

custodian of a minor One who manages a gift of securities to a minor under the Uniform Gifts to Minors Act (UGMA) or the Uniform Transfer to Minors Act (UTMA).

day order An order that is canceled if it is not executed on the day it is entered.

debenture A debt obligation backed by the general credit of the issuing corporation.

debt service The annual amount needed to pay interest and principal (or the scheduled sinking fund contribution) on an outstanding debt.

debt-to-equity ratio The ratio of total debt to total stockholder's equity.

default The failure to pay interest or principal promptly when due.

defeasance When a corporation or municipality removes debt from its balance sheet by issuing a new debt issue or creating a trust to be funded by assets, typically U.S. government securities that will generate enough cash flow to provide for the payment of interest and principal on the debt issue removed from the balance sheet (refunded).

deflation A persistent fall in the general level of prices.

demand-pull A type of inflation resulting from an excessive money supply that increases the demand for goods (i.e., too much money chasing too few goods).

discount rate The interest rate charged to member banks that borrow from the nine Federal Reserve Banks.

dividend A distribution of earnings of a corporation. Dividends may be in the form of cash, stock or property (securities owned by a corporation).

dividend payout ratio   A ratio used to analyze a company's policy of paying cash dividends, calculated by dividing the dividends paid on common stock by the net income available for common stockholders.

DNR   *See* do not reduce order.

dollar cost averaging   For mutual funds, a system of buying fixed dollar amounts of securities at regular fixed intervals, regardless of the price of the shares. This method may result in an average cost that is generally lower than the average price of all prices at which the securities were purchased.

do not reduce order (DNR)   An order that stipulates that the price of limit or stop orders should not be reduced as a result of cash dividends.

earnings per share (EPS)   The net income available for common stock divided by the number of shares of common stock outstanding.

economic risk   The risk related to international developments and domestic events.

endorsement   The signature on the back of a certificate by the person named on the certificate as owner. Owner(s) must endorse certificates when selling or transferring them to another person.

EPS   *See* earnings per share.

equity   The ownership interest of common and preferred stockholders in a corporation; also, the client's net worth in a margin account; also, what is owned less what is owed. *See also* common stock, margin account.

excess equity   The amount of money in a margin account that is in excess of the federal requirement.

face value   *See* par value.

Fed call   *See* margin call.

federal call   *See* margin call.

FIFO   *See* first in, first out.

first in, first out (FIFO)   An accounting method for assessing a company's inventory in which it is assumed that the first goods acquired are the first to be sold. Also used to designate the order in which sales or withdrawals from an investment are made to de-

termine cost basis for tax purposes. *See also* last in, first out.

fiscal policy   The federal tax and spending policies set by Congress or the White House.

flat   A term used to describe bonds traded without accrued interest. The bonds are traded at the agreed upon market price only.

full faith and credit bond   *See* general obligation bond.

fundamental analysis   A method of securities analysis that tries to evaluate the intrinsic value of a particular stock. It is a study of the overall economy, industry conditions and the financial condition and management of a particular company.

general obligation bond (GO)   A type of municipal bond backed by the full faith, credit and taxing power of the issuer for payment of interest and principal. (*Syn.* full faith and credit bond)

general partner (GP)   A partner in a partnership who is personally liable for all debts of the partnership and who partakes in the management and control of the partnership.

GO   *See* general obligation bond.

good till canceled order (GTC)   An order that is left in force until it is executed or canceled. (*Syn.* open order)

GTC   *See* good till canceled order.

guardian   A person who manages a gift of securities to a minor under the Uniform Gifts to Minors Act (UGMA) or the Uniform Transfer to Minors Act (UTMA); also, a person who takes charge of an incompetent's affairs.

house maintenance call   *See* maintenance call.

house requirement   The minimum amount of equity that a client must maintain in a margin account according to the particular firm's rules (most firms have a higher maintenance requirement than that set by the NYSE).

individual retirement account (IRA)   A qualified tax-deferred retirement plan for employed individuals that allows a contribution for 100 percent of earned income up to a maximum of $2,000 per year. Some or all of the contribution may be tax-deductible, depending on the individual's compensation level and coverage by other qualified retirement plans.

inflation An increase in the general level of prices.

initial margin requirement The amount of equity a customer must deposit when making a new purchase in a margin account. The Regulation T requirement is currently 50 percent for equity securities. The NYSE and NASD initial requirement is an equity of $2,000, but not more than 100 percent of the purchase cost. *See also* margin account.

initial public offering (IPO) A company's initial public offering, sometimes referred to as *going public,* is the first sale of stock by the company to the public.

investment banker A financial professional who raises capital for corporations and municipalities.

IPO *See* initial public offering.

IRA *See* individual retirement account.

joint tenants in common (JTIC) A form of ownership directing that upon the death of one tenant, the decedent's fractional interest in the joint account be retained by his or her estate. This form of ownership may be used by any two or more individuals.

joint tenants with right of survivorship (JTWROS) A form of ownership that requires that a deceased tenant's fractional interest in an account be retained by the surviving tenant(s). It is used almost exclusively by husbands and wives. *See also* joint tenants in common.

JTIC *See* joint tenants in common.

JTWROS *See* joint tenants with right of survivorship.

last in, first out (LIFO) A method assessing a company's inventory in which it is assumed that the goods acquired last are the first to be sold. Also used to designate the order in which sales or withdrawals from an investment are made to determine cost basis for tax purposes. *See also* first in, first out.

legislative risk The risk associated with the impact of changes in laws on investment.

LIFO *See* last in, first out.

limited partner (LP) A partner who does not participate in the management or control of a partnership and whose liability for partnership debts is limited to the amount he or she invested in the partnership.

limit order A customer's order with instructions to buy a specified security below a certain price or sell a specified security above a certain price.

maintenance call A brokerage firm's demand that a client deposit money or securities when the client's equity falls below either the brokerage firm's minimum maintenance requirement or the higher maintenance call set by the NYSE. *See also* house maintenance call, NYSE maintenance requirement.

maintenance requirement *See* NYSE maintenance requirement.

margin account An account in which a brokerage firm lends a client part of the purchase price of securities. *See also* Regulation T.

margin call A demand for a client to deposit money or securities when a purchase is made in a margin account. *See also* initial margin requirement. (*Syn.* Fed call, federal call, Reg T call)

margin risk The risk that an investor will be required to deposit additional cash if his or her security positions are subject to adverse price movements.

market maker (principal) A dealer willing to accept the risk of holding securities to facilitate trading in a particular security or securities.

market order An order that is to be executed at the best available price.

market risk That risk due to day-to-day fluctuations in prices at which securities can be bought or sold.

market value The price at which an investor will buy or sell each share of common stock or each bond at a given time. Market value is determined by the interaction between buyers and sellers in the market.

maturity date The date on which the principal is repaid to the investor. *See also* par value.

monetary policy The policies and actions of the Federal Reserve Board that determine the rate of growth and the size of the money supply, which in turn affect interest rates.

mortgage bond A debt obligation secured by a property pledge. Mortgage bonds are liens or mortgages against the issuing corporation's properties and real estate assets.

NAV *See* net asset value.

net asset value (NAV) The value of an investment company share (or unit trust unit), calculated by deducting the fund's liabilities from the total assets of the portfolio and dividing this amount by the number of shares (units) outstanding. This is calculated once a day, based on the closing market price for each security in the fund's portfolio.

net change The difference between the closing price on the trading day reported and the previous day's closing price. In over-the-counter transactions, the term refers to the difference between the closing bids.

net worth The amount by which assets exceed liabilities. (*Syn.* shareholders' equity)

New York Stock Exchange maintenance call *See* NYSE maintenance call.

New York Stock Exchange maintenance requirement *See* NYSE maintenance requirement.

nine bond rule The NYSE rule that requires orders for listed bonds in quantities of nine bonds or fewer to be sent to the floor of the NYSE before being traded in the over-the-counter market.

NYSE maintenance call A demand for a client to deposit money or securities if the client's equity falls below the NYSE minimum maintenance level. *See also* equity.

NYSE maintenance requirement The minimum amount of equity that must be maintained in a margin account at all times according to NYSE rules. The present minimum maintenance for corporate securities is 25 percent of the current market value for a long position.

odd lot Less than the normal unit of trading, which is fewer than 100 shares of stock or five bonds.

offer An indication by an investor, a trader or a dealer of a willingness to sell a security or commodity. *See also* bid. (*Syn.* ask, quotation, quote)

offering price With mutual funds, the price an investor will pay per share. The offering price is the net asset value plus a sales charge (for funds that have a sales charge).

OID *See* original issue discount.

open order *See* good till canceled order.

original issue discount (OID) A bond issued at a discount from face value at maturity. The bond may or may not pay interest, and the discount is taxed as if accrued annually as ordinary income. (*Syn.* stripped bonds)

outstanding stock Issued stock minus treasury stock (stock reacquired by the issuing corporation); stock that is in the hands of the public.

overbought A technical analyst's opinion that more and stronger buying has occurred in a market than the market fundamentals would justify.

oversold A technical analyst's opinion that more and stronger selling has occurred in a market than the market fundamentals would justify.

par value An arbitrary dollar value assigned to each share of stock at the time of issuance; the principal amount (face value) of a bond on which interest is calculated. *See also* maturity date.

PE *See* price-earnings ratio.

PE ratio *See* price-earnings ratio.

Pink Sheets The daily quotation sheets that publish the interdealer wholesale quotes for over-the-counter stocks.

portfolio income The income from interest, dividends and other nonbusiness investments.

price-earnings ratio (PE) The ratio of the current market value of the stock divided by the annual earnings per share.

primary offering An offering in which the proceeds of the underwriting (either equity or debt) go to the issuing corporation or municipality. A corporation increases its capitalization by selling stock (either a new issue or a previously authorized but unissued stock). It may do this at any time and in any amount, provided the total stock outstanding never exceeds the amount authorized in the corporation's bylaws. A municipality raises money by issuing debt.

principal transaction A transaction in which a broker-dealer or bank dealer buys stocks or bonds from customers and takes them into its own inventory. It then sells stocks or bonds to customers from its inventory.

prospectus The legal document that must be given to every investor who purchases registered securities in an offering. It describes the details of the company and the particular offering. (*Syn.* final prospectus)

proxy To vote on corporate matters, a stockholder must attend the annual meeting. If the stockholder is unable to attend, he or she may vote by proxy. A proxy is given in writing, authorizing another to vote for the stockholder according to the stockholder's instructions.

public offering *See* initial public offering.

public offering price (POP) The price of new shares that is established in the issuing corporation's prospectus; also, the price to investors for mutual fund shares.

quotation The bid and ask of a particular security.

quote (bond) Like stock quotes, bond prices are quoted in the financial press and most daily newspapers. Corporate bonds are quoted in ⅛ths. Government bonds are quoted in 1/32nds. The quotes for corporate and government bonds are percentages of the bonds' face value ($1,000). Municipal bonds may be quoted on a dollar basis or on a yield to maturity.

quote (stock) Many stocks traded are quoted in the financial press and most daily newspapers. A stock is quoted in points, with each point equal to $1. The price of the stock is further broken down into ⅛ths of a point, where ⅛ equals 12.5 cents.

range A security's low price and high price for a particular trading period (e.g., close of the day's trading, opening of the day's trading, day, month, year).

real estate investment trust (REIT) An investment trust that operates through the pooled capital of many investors who buy its shares. Investments are direct ownership of either income property or mortgage loans.

realized gain The amount of gain the taxpayer actually incurred on the sale or other disposition of property.

realized loss The amount of loss the taxpayer actually incurred on the sale or other disposition of property.

redemption notice A notice that a company or municipality is redeeming (or calling) a certain issue of bonds.

refunding A method of retiring an outstanding bond issue using the money from the sale of a new offering. This may occur before maturity (advance refunding) or at maturity (refunding).

registered bond A bond on which the name of the owner appears on the certificate.

registrar An independent organization or part of a corporation charged with the responsibility of seeing that the corporation does not have more stock outstanding than is accounted for on the corporation's books.

Reg T call *See* margin call.

regular way A settlement contract that calls for delivery and payment on the third business day following the date of trade. This is the usual type of settlement. For government securities, regular way is the next business day.

Regulation T The Federal Reserve Board regulation governing the credit that brokerage firms and dealers may extend to clients for the purchase of securities. Regulation T also governs cash accounts.

Regulation U The Federal Reserve Board regulation governing loans by banks for the purchase of securities.

reinvestment Reinvesting mutual fund distributions (dividends and gains) in the fund to purchase additional shares instead of receiving the distributions in cash.

REIT *See* real estate investment trust.

retiring bonds The act of calling bonds by a notice in the newspaper, by purchasing bonds in the open market or by repaying bondholders the principal amount at maturity.

revenue bond A bond whose interest and principal are payable only from specific earnings of an income-producing (revenue-producing) enterprise.

right of accumulation The right to qualify for reduced sales loads based on the dollar position held by the investor in a mutual fund.

scale Important data concerning each of the scheduled maturities in a new serial bond issue, including the number of bonds, date, maturity, coupon rate and offering price.

secured bond A bond backed by some form of collateral. In the event the company defaults on payment, the bondholders may attach the collateral backing the bond.

Series EE bond A nonmarketable U.S. government savings bond issued at a discount from par.

Series HH bond A nonmarketable interest-bearing U.S. government savings bond issued at par.

settlement date The date on which a transaction must be settled (exchange of cash for securities).

short sale The sale of a security that the seller does not own or any sale consummated by the delivery of a security borrowed by or for the account of the seller.

sinking fund A fund established by a corporation or municipality into which money is regularly deposited so that the corporation or municipality has the funds to redeem its bonds, debentures or preferred stock.

spot market A market in which goods are traded for immediate delivery and immediate payment.

stock ahead A limit order at a specific price that is not filled because other orders at that same price were entered before that limit order.

stock dividend *See* dividend.

stock power A standard form that duplicates the back of a stock certificate. It is used if the registered owner of a security does not have

the certificate available for signature endorsement.

stock split A reduction in the par value of stock caused by the issuance of additional stock. A reverse split increases the stock's par value by reducing the number of shares outstanding.

stop order An order that becomes a market order when the market price of the security reaches or exceeds the specific price stated in the stop order.

street name Securities held by a brokerage firm in its own name but owned by the client are referred to as being held in street name.

stripped bond A bond stripped of its coupons, repackaged and sold at a deep discount and maturing at full face value.

subordinated debenture A debt obligation that has unsecured junior claims to interest and principal subordinated to ordinary debentures and all other liabilities of the issuing corporation. *See also* debenture.

technical analysis A method of securities analysis that analyzes statistics generated by market activity, such as past prices and volume. Technical analysis does not attempt to measure a security's intrinsic value.

tenants in common (TIC) *See* joint tenants in common (JTIC).

tender offer An offer to buy securities for cash or for cash and securities.

term bond *See* term maturity

term maturity A type of maturity in which the entire bond issue matures on a single date. (*Syn.* term bond)

TIC *See* tenants in common.

trade date The date on which a transaction occurs.

transfer agent A person or an organization responsible for recording the names of the registered stockholders and the number of shares owned, seeing that the certificates are signed by the appropriate corporate officers, affixing the corporate seal and delivering the securities to the transferee.

trendline The line that traces a stock's movement by connecting the reaction lows in an upward trend or the rally highs in a downward trend.

trust indenture The written agreement between a corporation and its creditors that details the term of the debt issue. These terms include such things as the rate of interest, maturity date, means of payment and collateral.

UGMA *See* Uniform Gifts to Minors Act.

underwriting manager The brokerage firm responsible for organizing a syndicate, preparing the issue, negotiating with the issuer and underwriters and allocating stock to the selling group. (*Syn.* manager, manager of the syndicate, managing underwriter)

Uniform Gifts to Minors Act (UGMA) The act that permits gifts of money and securities to be given to minors and allows adults to act as custodians for minors.

Uniform Transfer to Minors Act (UTMA) The act that permits gifts of money and securities to be transferred to minors and allows adults to act as custodians for minors.

unrealized gain The amount of gain the taxpayer has achieved on paper for a position currently held.

unrealized loss The amount of loss the taxpayer has achieved on paper for a position currently held.

unsecured bond *See* debenture.

UTMA *See* Uniform Transfer to Minors Act.

wash sale The purchase of the same (or a substantially identical) security within 30 days before or after the sale establishing a loss. The claimed loss will be disallowed.

when issued security (WI) A security offered for sale in advance of the security's issuance by the issuer.

WI *See* when issued security.

zero-coupon bond *See* original issue discount, stripped bond.

Index